Praise for
Living in Love

"This is a terrific book on marriage from two people who know what they're talking about. They have earned the right to speak, and we are blessed indeed to listen."

    —BETH MOORE, author of *So Long, Insecurity: You've Been a Bad Friend to Us*

"James and Betty must know something. Spend any moments near them, and you quickly detect, and enjoy, an uncommon affection. I pray that we learn from their experience."

    —MAX LUCADO, pastor and best-selling author

"It has been said a good marriage is a blessing to the world. I do believe those who read their book will find this to be true in James and Betty's own union. We can all learn from their experience, and we thank them for that."

    —ROBERT DUVALL, actor

"We appreciate the way James and Betty Robison relate to each other with such respect and dignity. They are the same people on- and off-camera, and that is the test of a quality marriage. We know you will love Living in Love, because here they reveal the secrets behind their beautiful story and great marriage."

    —JOHN and STASI ELDREDGE, authors of *Captivating: Unveiling the Mystery of a Woman's Soul* and *Love and War: Finding the Marriage You've Dreamed Of*

"In today's world, I know of no better countercultural act that Christians can do than demonstrate faithfulness and joy in marriage. We all enter marriage believing it will last, but, sadly, it often doesn't. James and Betty don't just diagnose the problems but give practical steps for solving them."

    —PHILIP YANCEY, author of *What's So Amazing About Grace?*

"I've known James and Betty Robison for years, and they're the real deal. Their book is more than the real deal. They were so vulnerable in sharing their own struggles. Anyone who has ever asked themselves "Is this marriage working? Is it worth it?" will embrace this book and will embrace James and Betty as they share from the heart God's plan for marriage. What a great job they did on this book!"

—Dr. Kevin Leman, *New York Times* best-selling author of *Have a New Kid by Friday*, *Have a New Husband by Friday*, and *Have a New You by Friday*

"James and Betty are one of the couples I love and admire most in this world. I have had the joy of sharing many meals and deep conversations with them and always come away richer and closer to Christ. In a world where relationships are crumbling at an unprecedented rate, James and Betty share what they have lived and continue to live. This wisdom is priceless!"

—Sheila Walsh, author and Women of Faith speaker

"James and Betty Robison do a fine job teaching together and making their book on the challenges of marriage come alive. The honesty, the transparency, and the practical biblical insights and application make this book easy to understand. It will make a great gift for anyone in a marriage or soon to be wed."

—Dr. Charles Stanley, senior pastor, First Baptist Atlanta, and founder and president, In Touch Ministries

"In Living in Love, James and Betty Robison share their fifty-year endearing love story of hope, commitment, endurance, perseverance, and passion. Their marriage is a real-life example of what living out a covenant marriage looks like. Their testimony challenges us to the core, continually reminding us to press on in our marriage and never give up."

—Jeff and Cheryl Scruggs, authors of *I Do Again: How We Found a Second Chance at Our Marriage—and You Can Too*

"I cannot think of anyone more equipped to write a book on marriage than James and Betty Robison. Along with my own parents' marriage, theirs has made an indelible imprint on my life. As we've shared dinner and conversations, I've been enthralled to watch their adoring smiles, caring touches, and intimate exchanges. Indeed, this is a marriage to behold. I'm so glad they've chosen to give insight that will help us all build solid marriages of our own. Read and be blessed."

—Priscilla Shirer, author and Bible teacher

"James and Betty are an authentic couple who have a tremendous heart for God and a great love for each other. My wife, Katie, and I can tell by being around them how much they enjoy each other's company. The personal examples in Living in Love illustrate that they are a real couple dealing with real challenges. They let God's light shine through their marriage and demonstrate that, with God, couples can work through anything."

—Josh Hamilton, all-star outfielder of the Texas Rangers

"James and Betty Robison have provided every married couple with a solid tool to develop and maintain a marriage that will stand the test of time, trouble, trials, and tribulations. Living in Love is a must-read for couples who believe that God knew what He was doing when He created marriage and who want to see that purpose worked out in their own relationship."

—Tony and Lois Evans, Oak Cliff Bible Fellowship, Dallas

"As their pastor, I know that James and Betty Robison are authentic, sincere, and humble servants of the Lord, and they are most definitely and truly living in love. This book contains the keys you need for an exciting and fulfilling marriage. It has been a tremendous blessing to my wife, Debbie, and me, and I wholeheartedly recommend Living in Love for every couple."

—Robert Morris, senior pastor, Gateway Church, Southlake, Texas

"I've seen the marriage of James and Betty Robison up close and personal for over thirty years. Living in Love is from their heart. They have a happy partnership, which has led to a worldwide ministry, yet they have kept their marriage centered on Christ. They have struggled with many of the same issues you and I have confronted, and in this book they share what has worked for them. I highly recommend Living in Love."

—RUTH GRAHAM, author of *Fear Not Tomorrow, God Is Already There*

"This is not a book of just suggestions that might work. It is two lives joined together in love by practicing principles that will work—for any couple! Readers will be inspired by James and Betty's journey."

—DR. GARY SMALLEY, author of *From Anger to Intimacy*

"I have known James and Betty Robison for years, and I so enjoy being around them. That's because they always treat each other with love, respect, compassion, and good humor. Their book Living in Love tells us how to do the same. They didn't come by their great marriage automatically; they worked at it. And they learned valuable information along the way that they want to impart to others. Their personal story will touch you, and their insight will ignite you. This well-written book should be read by every married couple and also by anyone who hopes to be married in the future. I couldn't put it down."

—STORMIE OMARTIAN, author of *The Power of a Praying Wife* and *The Power of a Praying Husband*

JAMES & BETTY
ROBISON

LIVING *in* Love

Co-hosts of TV's *LIFE Today*, James & Betty
Share Keys *to an* Exciting *and* Fulfilling Marriage

WATERBROOK
PRESS

LIVING IN LOVE
PUBLISHED BY WATERBROOK PRESS
12265 Oracle Boulevard, Suite 200
Colorado Springs, Colorado 80921

All Scripture quotations, unless otherwise indicated, are taken from the Holy Bible, New Living Translation, copyright © 1996, 2004, 2007. Used by permission of Tyndale House Publishers Inc., Wheaton, Illinois 60189. All rights reserved. Scripture quotations are taken from the Amplified® Bible. Copyright © 1954, 1958, 1962, 1964, 1965, 1987 by The Lockman Foundation. Used by permission. (www.Lockman.org). Scripture quotations marked (NASB) are taken from the New American Standard Bible®. © Copyright The Lockman Foundation 1960, 1962, 1963, 1968, 1971, 1972, 1973, 1975, 1977, 1995. Used by permission. (www.Lockman.org). Scripture quotations marked (NIV) are taken from the Holy Bible, New International Version®, NIV®. Copyright © 1973, 1978, 1984 by Biblica Inc.™ Used by permission of Zondervan. All rights reserved worldwide. www.zondervan.com. Scripture quotations marked (NKJV) are taken from the New King James Version®. Copyright © 1982 by Thomas Nelson Inc. Used by permission. All rights reserved.

ISBN 978-0-307-72987-3
ISBN 978-0-307-45919-0 (electronic)

Edited by Dave Lindstedt and Bruce Nygren
Cover photo copyright © 2009 by David Dobson

Published in the United States by WaterBrook Multnomah, an imprint of the Crown Publishing Group, a division of Random House Inc., New York.

WATERBROOK and its deer colophon are registered trademarks of Random House Inc.

The Library of Congress cataloged the hardcover edition as follows:
Robison, James, 1943-
   Living in love : James & Betty share keys to an exciting and fulfilling marriage / James and Betty Robison. — 1st ed.
      p. cm.
   Includes bibliographical references.
   ISBN 978-1-4000-7458-7 — ISBN 978-0-307-45919-0 (electronic)
   1. Marriage—Religious aspects—Christianity. I. Robison, Betty. II. Title.
   BV835.R59 2010
   248.8'44—dc22

                            2010010185

Printed in the United States of America
2011—First Trade Paperback Edition

10 9 8 7 6 5 4 3 2 1

SPECIAL SALES
Most WaterBrook Multnomah books are available at special quantity discounts when purchased in bulk by corporations, organizations, and special-interest groups. Custom imprinting or excerpting can also be done to fit special needs. For information, please e-mail SpecialMarkets@WaterBrookMultnomah.com or call 1-800-603-7051.

◆ ◆ ◆

We dedicate this book to our three children,
Rhonda, Randy, and Robin,
and their spouses,
Terry, Debbie, and Kenny,
who are wonderful examples
of living in love.

CONTENTS

PART 4: *Challenges*

Introduction

JAMES

*J*ust in case you think Betty and I have a perfect relationship, let me share a story.

Before we started writing this book, we filmed a series on marriage for our *Life Today* television program. And of course, the night before we were going to tape a segment on how to communicate well with your spouse, we had what Betty calls a "heated discussion." After we calmed down, I told her, "We'll probably file for divorce while we're teaching about love and marriage!" We laughed about it…kinda.

After nearly fifty years together, we still face frequent moments that test our communication and relationship. And it always seems to happen that we come under pressure anytime we try to help others.

As is often the case in marriage, our heated discussion started around a minor issue, something Betty had said to me about my performance on a plumbing repair at the house. I had worked all day to fix a toilet that wasn't working right, because I thought doing this would really make her happy. But after hours of toiling, I still couldn't get the blooming thing to work. I had even used duct tape, which every real repairperson knows fixes almost anything!

So while I was still in the middle of my plumbing challenge, Betty came by and said, "I'd just like to be able to go to the bathroom in *this bathroom*, since it's the master bathroom!"

I found this statement offensive and shot back, not so sweetly, "Well, we've got another one in the house. Go use that one!" Betty gave me a less than complimentary look but didn't respond.

After my feelings about her "insensitive" remark subsided, I got the brilliant idea to go to that other bathroom and see if it had the same make and model toilet. Sure enough it did, so I dismantled it and got the parts I needed to fix the first commode. After only a few minutes, I had the toilet put together and working like a charm. Feeling like a rocket scientist, I said excitedly, "Betty, I fixed it!"

"Well, you need to get that other toilet you took the parts from fixed too!" she answered.

That wasn't the response I was looking for, and I got angry all over again. "I cannot believe I did all that work, and now you're going to lecture me about a toilet that a month from now somebody might use."

That started our discussion!

✦ BETTY

And it was a loud one! I knew it wasn't a very nice thing to say to him. So I apologized. We do vent our feelings and air our laundry, but God's Spirit enables us to have a sensitivity and respect for each other that allows us to stay committed and able to forgive and move on as a team.

But it took us a long time to get to this point. When we first married, I was a very good pouter. I didn't want to confront James with anything, because I didn't feel I had strong enough words to present my case. Over time I recognized the foolishness of not dealing with disagreements and misunderstandings and misstatements.

You may be thinking, Oh, you don't have any idea what serious problems look like! All you argued about was a toilet that needed to be fixed?

I agree that arguing about a toilet may seem trite, but often it is the little things that mount up if you don't communicate about them and confront each other. Then they build up into a mountain, and the heart hardens, making it difficult to resolve more serious issues. And believe me, we've had more serious issues.

You need a sensitivity to each other that can come only from God. And when you approach a confrontation with a humble attitude, you just don't know what that might do for your relationship. It may open up the closed-off heart of the other person.

✦ JAMES

I know this was a silly thing—a broken toilet—but what Betty said hurt me because I felt dissed. I felt like what I had accomplished wasn't appreciated.

✦ BETTY

I apologized because I realized I had not shown appreciation for James's hard work.

✦ JAMES

What was so meaningful about that heated discussion was that, because our confrontation was respectful and not accusatory, literally in only a few minutes, I was sitting in front of Betty, looking at her, and saying, "Is this not cool?"

What I meant is that over the years we have learned how to handle both serious and silly situations like this without Betty's going off to pout and my getting upset because we could not immediately settle the issue. We have learned how to communicate, vent, and openly share our hearts. We know it's important to hear what the other person's heart is saying, not just the words coming from his or her mouth.

Betty and I have learned, and we are continuing to learn, to confront each other with the right attitude. We now know how to approach each other, not with a spirit of "I'm going to straighten you out," but rather, "Hey, I really may need to change because I don't understand this, and I need you to help me."

Ultimately, this is about placing our relationship, conflicts and all, before God and letting Him heal us.

✦ BETTY

The reason we've written this book is that many people say to us, "It seems that you two are really happy as a couple. What are the keys to your happiness?" The best answer we can give is found in the pages that follow. We invite you to join us for an extended discussion of what it takes to make a marriage that truly is sweeter every day.

✦ JAMES

After nearly fifty years we still have serious and, yes, heated discussions, but we enjoy an exhilarating, truly fulfilling marriage relationship. I believe with all my heart that the insights we share in this book can have a very positive impact on all your relationships and certainly on your marriage. Betty and I pray that you'll not be distracted or put this book aside but that you'll allow us to share what we have discovered, because it is possible to *live in love*.

PART I

Beginnings

1

Expectations

They make or break a marriage.

JAMES

When Betty and I married, like every couple, we had certain hopes, dreams, and expectations. I was looking for love and someone to share my life with who really cared about me. Betty was looking for love, security, a family, and a home. Even more critically, in some ways she was looking for her identity.

I'm sure the same is true for you. When you decided to get married, you obviously felt it was worth dedicating your life to. You desired lifelong happiness, joy, and peace with your spouse, and you committed yourselves to each other with your actions, your emotions, and your words. And you both had certain expectations that your needs would be met by this other person with whom you were so deeply in love.

I like to illustrate this point by telling of a journey Betty and I took with our son, Randy, one autumn to see the beauty of the aspens as they changed colors in the Rocky Mountains of Colorado. To get to a spot that offered a great view, we had to drive on a steep, narrow mountain road that twisted and turned as it climbed through the Rockies. The traffic was extremely heavy. Randy was at the wheel, and without warning the car began to vibrate. He fought to keep the car on the road as it tried to veer right, toward a concrete barrier. There was no shoulder to the roadway, just a retaining wall, so Randy stopped the car safely in the middle of our lane. We realized then that we'd had a blowout on our right front tire, and now we were stuck. Traffic was flowing steadily to our left, and to the right a long line of cars was merging onto the highway just ahead of us. But an immediate danger came from our being stopped in the middle of the road. What if someone hit us from behind?

And then a miracle happened. Instead of an eighteen-wheeler bearing down on us with no chance of stopping, a police car pulled up behind us. The officer parked his car at an angle and turned on his flashing lights to alert drivers approaching from the rear that they had to go around us. The policeman stayed there the entire time we were stuck and protected us from harm.

Here's my point: Maybe you have a great marriage, or maybe your marriage is suffering. Maybe you're single and praying that God will send the right person your way. Maybe you're engaged and wondering what you're getting into. Regardless of whether you are in or out of a relationship, you have some ideas of what a marriage should look like.

When you get married, you expect it to be a wonderful journey. You expect to see the most beautiful things that life has to offer, like the stunning autumn leaves we were on our way to view in Colorado. But I can guarantee that somewhere along the way your relationship will stop running smoothly. Maybe you'll have a blowout or maybe just a slow leak. But eventually you'll have a flat tire on your marriage journey.

The challenge to your relationship might come on a winding mountain road, on an eight-lane superhighway, or on the neighborhood streets of daily life. But no matter where or when it happens, an unexpected test always comes.

Will you fall into worry about being hit by traffic and get so worked up that you can't do anything to fix the problem? That's just going to get you run over.

Will you try to ignore the problem and keep going?

Will you get mad and blame the car for not moving you forward? That would be pointless anger.

Or will you trust the Protector, who's looking out for your marriage, and take the necessary action to get your relationship back on track?

Only you can decide.

When our tire blew out on that mountain road, we quickly realized that we had to get it fixed. And even though a policeman was protecting us, he couldn't fix the tire for us—we had to do it ourselves.

Because of the circumstances on that mountain road, we had trouble getting the spare tire out, so we wound up having our car hauled to a tire store. The police officer followed us all the way there.

As it turned out, it was a good thing we went to that tire store. When the manager looked at the other tires on our car, he noticed they were all worn and the sidewalls were weather cracked, conditions which were difficult to detect without putting the car on a lift. The tires could have blown out at any time. In order to stay safe and get our car back on the road to see those marvelous autumn leaves, we had to replace all the tires.

Many people marry with high expectations about experiencing the various colors of life, but a blowout can endanger the entire journey. When you have a blowout in your marriage, you may need to go to a professional counselor to get the other tires in your relationship checked. Sometimes those tiny, undetected cracks create hazardous driving conditions.

Betty and I have always had a commitment to see things through, no matter what. You may be in a great relationship like that, or you may feel as if you've compromised. You may think that you've brought too much baggage along or that the past mistakes of your partner are too great to overcome. Or you may feel as if the wheels have come off your marriage.

I'm telling you that with God on your side and with a heart-determined effort on your part, all things are possible. You can get your marriage relationship back on the road to fulfillment—even if you have to replace all four tires. With a clear commitment to God and to each other, you can learn how to endure the difficulties and trials of your relationship. You can come to realize that those challenges are not the end of your love; they are simply a new mountain you can climb, if you desire to do so. Instead of looking at your difficulties as ruts or roadblocks, view them as opportunities to make your marriage even better.

In God you have a Protector who has your best interests at heart, and helpers are available along the way to assist you in repairing all the damages in your marriage. Don't give up! If possible, find help before your relationship blows up. As you read this book, you will discover that all things are possible with God.

With God on your side and with a heart-determined effort on your part, all things are possible.

If you're at the beginning of your marriage or looking forward to the day when you will be married, we trust you will find some ingredients here, some building blocks that are critically important for establishing a thriving marriage from the get-go.

If you've been married for several years, let me encourage you that real change is still possible and improvement is sheer joy. The essential components of a thriving marriage can be put in place *at any point* and *at any time* in a marriage relationship. If you're willing to do what it takes, it's never too late to start doing the right thing…and enjoy living in love.

FOR REFLECTION AND DISCUSSION

What were your expectations for your marriage?

What challenges or potential blowouts do you see in your relationship?

How do you want to apply the promise "All things are possible with God" in your marriage?

2

Boy Meets Girl:
How James Met Betty

Opposites really do attract!

JAMES

From all outward appearances, Betty and I never should have gotten together. We came from two different worlds with two very different life experiences. Hers was more typical and stable; mine was the complete opposite.

Growing up, I had no father and no family. Born to an impoverished, forty-one-year-old woman as the result of a forced sexual relationship, I came into this world in a charity ward. Because my mother did not have the means to care for a child, she sought foster care for me by placing an ad in a Houston newspaper.

A Southern Baptist pastor and his wife, Rev. Doyle and Katie Hale of Pasadena, Texas, took me in and gave me a secure home for the first five years of my life, but then my mother came back to reclaim me. She was so destitute she didn't have the money for bus fare when she picked me up. But not wanting the Hales to know her true condition and not wanting to ask them for help, she took me on a city bus across town, and then we hitchhiked to Austin, where I lived for the next ten very difficult years.

I believe my mother loved me and wanted the best for me, but her own life was so unstable and uncertain that she simply didn't have the resources to give me proper care. We moved so often during those years that the concept of home had no meaning for me. My mother would often leave me with other people—many of whom I didn't know. Even now I clearly remember spending hours staring out a window and wondering if she would come back for me. It certainly wasn't the best way to learn about commitment, trust, and love. Everything I knew about relationships was programmed into me the wrong way.

Betty, on the other hand, was reared in a fairly stable middle-class home with a quiet, nonexpressive father and a strong mother, both of whom tried to give a sense of security to Betty and her brother and sisters. Betty grew up going to church twice every Sunday and on Wednesday and Thursday nights for prayer, evangelism, and visitation. She sang in the choir, taught a junior girls' Sunday school class, and often sang duets with her sister Helen. When I first met Betty, I thought she was the sweetest—and certainly the purest—girl I had ever seen.

The two of us seemed a very unlikely match, but God had other ideas. Before we explain how we learned to live in love, Betty and I want to share some background on how we met.

HOW WE MET: JAMES'S STORY

The summer when I was fourteen, I went to Pasadena to spend a couple of weeks with the Hales, the family who had taken me in as an infant. By being with the Hales, I was able to compare their lives and relationships to the dysfunction I saw in my own family and in the dilapidated neighborhoods of Austin where I lived. I noticed the difference in commitment—in their commitment to each other and to God—and it impressed me.

During those two weeks with my foster family, I realized that in order to experience real meaning in life, I needed to commit myself to God and to a life of purpose. During a Sunday night service, after hearing the moving testimonies of several teenagers and through the tearful witness of Mrs. Hale, I publicly committed my life to Christ. About a week later I went back to Austin and did my best over the next year to live as a Christian.

The two of us seemed a very unlikely match, but God had other ideas.

Around that same time, for reasons I never quite understood, my mother married my biological father, Joe Robison, the man who had forced himself on her fifteen years earlier while, as a practical nurse, she was caring for his elderly father. Suddenly this alcoholic man was in our lives, which only made things more difficult than they already had been. I didn't know my father at all, and when he was around, he was usually drunk. He had a temper, and I learned to avoid him.

The spring after my visit to the Hales, my father got drunk and worked himself into a rage. He wrapped his hands around my mother's throat and choked her. Only when she passed out did he finally release his grip, thinking she was dead. Passing out saved her life.

A few days later my father, drunk again, verbally threatened my life. In fear I ran to get my .30-caliber rifle, which I had purchased with the hope of someday going deer hunting. I pointed the barrel at my father's chest and said, "If you so much as move a finger, I'll blow a hole in you big enough for somebody to crawl through." I know I would have done it. I believe the only reason he stayed perfectly still, cursing me all the while, was because the Hales and many of their church members were praying for me. Never underestimate the power of prayer! If he had moved, I would have pulled the trigger, and my life would have changed forever. Only a supernatural power could have kept my father still.

The tense standoff ended when the sheriff responded to my call for help and took my father to jail. Soon after this horrific experience, I went back to

Pasadena to spend the summer with the Hales. And that's when everything began to change for the better.

My first Sunday back in Pasadena, I went to Memorial Baptist Church, where Reverend Hale was the pastor. Walking into the building through a side entrance, I was introduced to a brunette girl, about my age, wearing a yellow chiffon dress. My first impression was that she was cute and sweet, but I didn't dwell on this first encounter.

That evening, as I sat toward the back of the room during the Sunday night Bible study, I glanced several rows in front of me and saw the same girl, this time wearing a modest but flattering white dress and looking back at me with a transforming smile. I was spellbound by the dimples in her cheeks, the sparkle in her eyes, and her completely disarming innocence. But what I said to the boy next to me was, "She's got a great figure."

Her name was Betty Freeman. And I was captivated.

I saw Betty the following day at the church's Vacation Bible School, where both of us were helping the younger children as volunteers, and I gave her a ride home at lunchtime. Our first real date didn't occur until Wednesday, when I asked her out after the midweek prayer meeting. We went to the Grove, a popular drive-in similar to Sonic, to get a frosty mug of root beer. Later we spent some time talking in Reverend Hale's car, which he had loaned me for the occasion.

Having never been on a real date before, I didn't know that being alone in a car with a girl in an isolated location maybe wasn't the best idea. But since professing my faith in Christ the previous summer, I understood I had a new Father who said He was "well pleased" with me for accepting Jesus, and I was committed and determined to follow through with biblical purity and respect for this sweet girl I'd just met.

I hadn't grown up knowing God, but in the best way I knew how, I wanted His best for my life, including my relationships. Even as a boy I had determined that I wanted to marry a strong, uncompromising girl who had an obvious commitment to moral purity. I also wanted a girl who had a sweet spirit, and the more I talked to Betty, the sweeter I realized she was.

As we began to date, I showed respect for Betty and told her I wanted to guard her purity. But like any teenage boy, I wasn't above testing the limits, and I knew myself well enough to realize there probably would come a time when I would say anything to get Betty to give in. But I was honest with her about that, and I cautioned her not to compromise. I told her that I never wanted to lose the respect I had for her and that we would really have to help each other remain pure. This level of respect helped reveal to Betty how real Jesus was to me, and her heart's desire to remain pure told me a lot about her as well.

When I returned home after our first date, I knew I'd gone out with a girl who was special in every way. I went to the bedroom the Hales had prepared for me, closed the door, and knelt by my bed as tears welled up in my eyes. *Thank You, God, for letting me meet such a pure girl,* I prayed. *She's so special.*

HOW WE MET: BETTY'S STORY

♦ BETTY

I grew up the third of four children, and sometimes I felt as if I got lost in the shuffle. I wanted to be noticed and made to feel special, but I didn't want to rock the boat. I was very bashful, insecure, and fearful, and I didn't have a lot of self-esteem. I felt insignificant. I tried to be as good as I could be so I would never cause a problem or get in the way. I thought if I did everything right and obeyed all the rules, I would earn favor.

I knew my parents loved me, although my dad wasn't very affectionate or very expressive. I think I hungered for more affection from him, but I didn't get it. When I was older and knew more about his background, I understood why he wasn't more demonstrative: he had never received affection from his parents.

My mom was a more dominating person because, I think, my dad wouldn't lead in the home. She was forceful, and she intimidated me. I never felt very smart and was already pretty hard on myself. I struggled in school. Often I felt like hiding in a corner so no one would notice me and I wouldn't get criticized if I did something wrong. Mostly, I didn't want to disappoint anyone.

My older sister was a good student, and my mom gave her money whenever she earned straight A's, which she did quite often. Mother told me that if I made straight A's, then I would get some money too, but I never did. I worked at it and always did the best I could, but I would panic during tests and forget everything. So I felt I never met my mom's expectations. When I graduated from high school, I was just thankful I'd made it through.

When I was at church, though, I felt more accepted. I thought I could do good things there, and I liked being in that atmosphere and enjoyed the activities. My perspective on church was that if I did everything right and everything good, then God would love me; He'd accept me because of my good deeds. Even though I was a member of the church, I really didn't know Jesus.

When I met James, I was impressed. He was a good-looking guy and was so cool with his blue jeans, white T-shirt, and suntan. We hit it off right away and soon were spending most of our time together. He made me feel important and pretty, and I enjoyed being with him. My mom used to ask me if James didn't have someplace else he needed to be, because he was always at our house. We'd talk while I was doing my chores, and we got to know each other quite well that first summer, although James didn't talk much about his background. I think he wanted to put it behind him.

When the time came for James to return to Austin for the school year, he told the Hales he didn't want to go back. They assured him he was welcome to stay if he could get his mother's permission, but that seemed unlikely. She had cut off communication with the Hales after taking James back when he was five, and it was only after the incident with his father and the hunting rifle that she had allowed James to reconnect with them.

As I watched James and a friend of his board a Greyhound bus to return to

Austin, I began to pray—and prayed constantly—until I heard that he would be able to return. Two days later I rode with Reverend Hale to pick up James in Austin and bring him back to Pasadena for good.

James found it more difficult to leave Austin than he had imagined. His mother had left him a tear-stained note, saying she had cried all night. Her face was so puffy and blotchy from crying that she didn't want me to see her when Reverend Hale and I came to pick up James.

At the end of the summer, he enrolled at Pasadena High School as a junior, one year ahead of me.

Because I was very involved in church, I wanted James to love church as much as I did. He went to the activities to be with me, but because he was uncomfortable in crowds and group settings, he never became regularly involved in our church. He and I broke up once because I chose to go on a hayride with the youth group rather than on a date alone with him. But we were soon back together again.

The summer after James graduated from high school, I involved him in a weeklong series of revival meetings at the church, organized entirely by the youth group and featuring a dynamic sixteen-year-old evangelist, Daniel Vestal. At first James wasn't happy with me, because I had worked it out that he would accompany Daniel and introduce him from the platform each night. (Like me, James was shy and terrified of public speaking.) But the more time he spent with Daniel Vestal, hearing him quote Scripture and talk about the Bible and watching him preach powerful messages each night, the more James became inspired. By Friday night he had reached the point of making a life-changing decision about his future. I'll never forget sitting with the youth choir and hearing Reverend Hale announce to the assembly, "James feels that God has called him to be an evangelist."

Until then James had been extremely quiet and shy. But when God called him to preach, the transformation was so remarkable that we knew it was a miracle. His hunger for God's Word was kindled instantaneously, even more so than when he had become a Christian, and his confidence in speaking publicly was simply amazing. It was as if he couldn't hold it back.

Even though James hadn't come from a Christian background, he seemed to have something I was missing. He had his imperfections, certainly, but he also had a relationship with God that I didn't understand and didn't know if I could ever have. But it was so real and personal that I wanted it.

As James went to college and he and I continued to date, I saw the reality of Jesus in his life, and it caused me to reevaluate my own relationship with God. On one of our dates, as we discussed our faith, James said, "Jesus is as real to me as you are, sitting next to me."

That was when a light bulb turned on in my head. "Jesus is not that real to me," I said. "He's someone I've heard about all my life, but He isn't *real*." I had a church relationship but not a real relationship with Jesus. I had all the form but none of the fellowship.

One night after James and I had attended a Saturday night service at another church, I was convicted that I really didn't know Jesus in a personal way. Later, when James let me out at my house, he prayed with me and did not try to tell me whether I was saved or not. He said, "You just go in and talk to God." I was so deeply moved by God's Spirit that I had trouble going to sleep.

We decided early in our relationship that our commitment to God and to each other was imperative.

The next day was Sunday, and in the morning I went through my typical routine. I dressed for church, taught my junior girls' Sunday school class, went to the choir room and put on my robe, and sang in the choir. Then my sister and I walked to the pulpit and sang a duet as special music before the pastor preached. When he finished his sermon and gave an altar call, to everyone's amazement I came out of the choir—robe and all—walked down front, kneeled, and invited Jesus into my heart. I stood up, took the pastor's hand, and said, "Brother Hale, I just gave my life to Jesus!"

"Betty," he said, "you're the best girl in this church! What do you mean?"

"Please stop telling me how good I am," I said. "I'm tired of trying to be what I'm not. I just met Jesus."

After that, James and I moved to a new place in our relationship. We made a total commitment to God and to each other, and after four years of dating, we affirmed our commitment by getting engaged.

When James asked me to marry him, we were only nineteen years old and filled with dreams of our future together. I looked forward to a lifetime of giving my love to him and of sharing every part of my life with him, including my strengths and my weaknesses.

We decided early in our relationship that our commitment to God and to each other was imperative. How else would we learn to stand firm when the going got tough? If we were always backing away from difficulties, we would never succeed at anything.

We stand on that commitment to this day, nearly fifty years later. We know that without commitment, without those forces in our lives helping us stand strong, we cannot love each other fully. It has taken a lot of trial and error, but we've learned valuable lessons along the way.

FINDING A FULFILLING RELATIONSHIP

✦ JAMES

Betty and I know that our marriage is blessed, and we honestly and truly enjoy each other. If you've watched our inspirational talk program, *Life Today,* you've seen us interacting in a joyful manner, revealing not only our love for God but also our genuine, joy-filled love for each other. This expression isn't just a show we put on while the cameras are rolling; it's who we really are.

It hasn't always been that way. Like every couple, we've gone through some serious challenges in our marriage. In the process we've learned a lot of things about ourselves, about God, and about how to truly live in love. These are the things we want to share with you, because we believe it is possible for every couple to live in a joyful, love-filled relationship.

In the pages that follow, we will tell more of the story of how a pretty girl from a secure and loving family and a boy from an impoverished and dysfunctional background ended up with an incredible fifty-year love relationship. We hope you'll be able to see that no matter what your background is, no matter what has happened thus far in your marriage, you can have a thriving, growing, fulfilling relationship.

 FOR REFLECTION AND DISCUSSION

Take some time to recall how you met the love of your life.

In what ways are you and your spouse alike? In what ways are you completely different?

How has your commitment to God and to each other made a difference in your marriage?

Key Ingredients

What's in the heart is what really matters.

JAMES

etty and I are convinced, through personal experience and observation, that if you want to live in love and have a successful marriage, three qualities are essential: *commitment, communication,* and *cooperation.* Unless you and your spouse have a total commitment to each other, open and honest communication, and a willingness to work together, you're in for trouble.

From the day we were married until this very day, Betty and I have been determined to have a joy that nothing could destroy—no circumstance, no problem, no disappointment or failure. Not that we haven't faced challenges over the years, because we've certainly had our share. But through all the ups and downs, we've stayed committed to each other and have been willing to embrace another important concept: *change.*

Our journey of a joyful marriage has required continual transformation. When we first married, we didn't have a single glorious experience that has carried us through nearly a half century. No, the more God imprints us and affects us, the more we're *being* shaped and changed. At sixty-six years of age and after forty-seven years of marriage, both Betty and I believe we are still soft clay in the hands of a mighty God. We are determined to remain yielded in His shaping hands.

What is the current attitude of your heart? Do you need to become more pliable in God's hands? Have you become hardened by the heat and pressures of life? Or are you still soft and malleable, still willing and able to be changed by the Potter?

As Betty and I submit to the necessary changes in life, we don't impose them on each other. Instead, we embrace them, and that acceptance overflows into our relationship. We still get frustrated with each other and have discussions, even heated ones. Our marriage wasn't made in heaven, but it's a relationship that heaven's power is still shaping. And this same power can shape your marriage as well.

Let me give you a bonus tip at no extra charge: no matter how much you are tempted to scrutinize your spouse, it's more important that you *stay pliable yourself!*

We encourage you to yield yourself to instruction and training just as an Olympic athlete or a person working toward a professional goal would yield to the rigors and discipline of training. In any pursuit of excellence, you must submit to the processes of training, improvement, and change. We understand this in athletics and music and dance, but sometimes we forget the same principles apply to marriage.

DO YOU WANT TO GET WELL?

What do you really want for your marriage? Are you satisfied with the status quo, or do you want more?

A story from the life of Jesus relates to these questions. One day He encountered a disabled man at the pool of Bethesda.[1] This man had been an invalid for a long time—thirty-eight years—and was lying within sight of the pool and its restorative powers. But he had never found a way to get into the water at the proper time, when healing would occur.

When Jesus saw the man, He asked him an interesting question: "Would you like to get well?"

On the surface this seems like a silly question. Why wouldn't the man want to get well? But Jesus knew that with healing and restoration would come new responsibilities. Was the man willing to do what it would take to be healthy and stay healthy?

Here's where the story strikes close to home. If your marriage is something less than what you had hoped for or expected, do you wish to get well? Do you really want to communicate and work together better? Do you want to know each other better—physically and emotionally? Do you want to grow spiritually as a team so you can better advance the kingdom of God?

I'm certain you have ideas and suggestions for changes your spouse could make, but the "would you like to get well" question is not for your spouse. It's for *you*. Are *you* willing to change? Are *you* willing to do what it will take to pick up your marriage from the ground and get it moving forward again?

In our years together of life and ministry, Betty and I have observed firsthand what statistics reveal: many people—perhaps *most* people—are not happy in their marriages. They're simply hanging in there, keeping a stiff upper lip, and letting the rough end drag. Many people stay married only for the sake of their children or for some other reason, but they are not for one moment enjoying the relationship they're trying to hold on to.

This breaks my heart.

It also brings us back to the question that Jesus asked the man at the pool of Bethesda: "Would you like to get well?"

I believe it is possible to face every marriage challenge in true harmony of heart and to win the battle in every area. Whether your struggles are with money, sex, kids, parents, faith, or what color to paint the bedroom, God wants you to have success in your marriage. Don't misunderstand me: you will not always win instant victories, and some struggles may last until death. But you can be delivered from recurring defeat if you face those challenges with a commitment to God and to each other and communicate openly and honestly.

I've experienced some instantaneous deliverance at times in my life, and I like it that way! But most victories come progressively as we learn to train our appetites and tame our flesh. Discipline is a pain, but it's necessary for a meaningful life.

In this book we're going to ask you to be honest about yourself and the condition of your marriage. It's only when you honestly face reality that you can hope to be honest with your mate. Our desire is to offer you hope, encouragement, and a vision for how wonderfully blessed your marriage can be. In order to do that, we must be truthful with you about what it's going to take.

CHANGE BEGINS IN YOUR HEART

I know this may disappoint you greatly, but this book is not about changing your husband or your wife. No sirree! Nor is this about following ten rules or seven steps for a better marriage. Real, lasting change cannot be imposed from the outside. It has to happen inside of us. In the words of Jean Sulivan, a twentieth-century French writer and priest, "Unity can't be imposed from without.... Every message that does not ripen in the individual conscience is dead."[2]

I like that image of ripening, because it brings to mind the natural process that makes fruit edible and delicious. There are some external steps that can be taken to help fruit ripen—for example, ethylene gas is used to ripen bananas—but those procedures only mimic the natural, internal process of the fruit itself. The best fruit ripens on the vine or on the tree through a normal maturation process.

Growth in a marriage is very much like the ripening of fruit: it has to happen on the inside before it will ever be seen on the outside. Qualities like commitment, trust, and concern are all interior traits that cannot be imposed on a person or a marriage relationship. How would you force a husband or a wife to be trustworthy or caring? These types of things have to come from inside a person or a relationship before they can become the foundation for a thriving marriage.

Even after forty-seven years of marriage, I'm still committed to myself and my own interests, but I'm equally committed to Betty and to our relationship. I'm also committed to making the necessary changes to become a better husband and a better person. That's because I've learned that in looking beyond myself to the well-being of Betty and our relationship, I have the greater possibility of achieving my own dreams.

That's why this book is as much about your inner transformation as an individual as it is about what you as a couple can do to strengthen your marriage.

Ideally, you and your spouse will read this book together, but the starting place for change will always be in your own heart.

◆ BETTY

I agree that change has to start in your own heart. And I think that can look a little different for the husband and the wife. As a woman I've seen that it's easy to enter marriage with a mothering attitude: "I love him, but he has a lot of things that need changing, and I'm just the one to do it." Another temptation is to think that your husband isn't quite stepping up to his proper leadership role, that he's not quite as committed to God as he should be.

Because women naturally want to be helpful, they have a legitimate need to feel needed. Often they think, *I can help him change or perhaps even make him change.* Trust me, that rarely happens! If that's your attitude, you're starting off on the wrong foot. First, you're unlikely to succeed, and, second, if you do change your husband, it won't be the change you want. Then you really are in a mess. You will have actually positioned yourself in the leadership role, when, in fact, most women find their greatest peace, joy, and security when the husband leads wisely.

For example, if a wife bosses or nags her husband or puts him down because he's not spiritual enough, that's only going to make him draw back even more. I think I saw some of that in my parents. My mom thought she could make my dad feel ashamed to the point that he would want to take on more leadership and want to go to church with the family. But I believe it only made things worse.

The best way to help a husband? Pray for him. God has to be the One to change him or inspire him to be a godly leader.

The principle that meaningful change always begins with oneself actually applies to both husbands and wives. Before you start visualizing changes in your spouse, you need to allow God to change you. Then, when your spouse sees the genuine change in you, he or she will come to realize that a true heart change is desirable and beautiful to behold.

> *The best way to help a husband? Pray for him.*

Early in our marriage I could see James's imperfections (isn't it always easier to see flaws in someone else?), but I was determined to keep my own imperfections hidden. That was mostly out of fear—fear that I wouldn't be accepted or that I wouldn't be loved—but it manifested itself as pride.

For example, at church one day we were asked to write down some of our sins. I couldn't think of any of my own, so I wrote down James's failures. That's pretty arrogant, but that was my focus at the time. Until we can be honest with ourselves, until we can face our own shortcomings, sins, and failures, we'll be stifled (and I was), and we won't be able to go anywhere in our walk of faith.

As you read the following chapters, from time to time you may have to set aside a natural human tendency to ask, "But what if my spouse…" Of course there will be plenty of things for you and your spouse to work on together, but real change always begins with you and the transformation of your own heart.

When transformation and healing take place in the human heart, the result is always an overflowing of love, forgiveness, and reconciliation in relationship. Inner transformation will not only make you a better mate, but it will also make you an inspiration to your spouse.

Our desire is to connect with you at whatever point you are in your marriage and to show you what's possible. In other words, no matter where you are, we have a vision of where we believe you can go. Our hope is to show you enough from our relationship to cause you to want to get your own marriage on a solid footing.

 For Reflection and Discussion

What do you really want for your marriage?

How would you evaluate the commitment, communication, and cooperation in your relationship?

What are some changes you should consider that would help your marriage thrive? (Remember: it is always wise to look openly at your own life first.)

PART 2

Commitment

Committed to Each Other

The glue of marriage is unbreakable devotion.

JAMES

What does commitment in marriage mean to you?

Betty and I think of it as being sold out. Having our priorities right. Yielded. Forsaking all others. Laying ourselves down for the cause or the other person. Commitment by its very nature is exclusive. It creates boundaries and makes room for relationship.

✦ BETTY

Our commitment to each other was tested even before we were married.

When James and I announced our engagement in the autumn of 1962, we didn't have much money, but we planned to pay for the wedding mostly on our own. James was preaching, and I had a job as a mail clerk and telephone operator for an industrial supply company, so we had some income. My parents wanted to chip in a little, although they didn't have much to spare.

We set a wedding date for the following May, but as time went on and we began to make plans, we decided we wanted to move up the date to February.

When I told my mother, she was against it. She liked James and approved of our engagement, but I don't think she knew how to handle her feelings about losing her daughter to marriage, and the earlier date for our wedding made it feel more threatening. Because my father did not usually take the lead or speak up in decision making, Mother took charge and let her feelings be known. Her forceful personality had always intimidated me, so I wasn't certain how I should respond to her resistance to our plans. James began to chafe and decided this was an opportune moment for us to test the "leaving and cleaving" idea. It also was the first real test of our commitment to each other.

When Mother continued to counsel us against our plans, James faced the issue head-on. One night when he was over for supper, he said to my mother, very politely and respectfully, "Ma'am, I cannot let you be in charge of this relationship. You will not be in charge of our wedding or our marriage. This is what we want to do, and if we have to do it totally on our own, we will. And if there's no ceremony, it doesn't matter."

While firm, he was gracious, and we certainly didn't want to sever our relationship with my parents, but the time had come to change the nature of that relationship. We wanted an open door to their wise counsel, but we didn't want the open door to include intrusive control. What James did was a necessary step in cutting the apron strings.

Every couple should seek to maintain a good relationship with their parents but not at the expense of their own marriage. We had to leave in order to cleave.

My mother wasn't accustomed to such a strong male response to her opinions, and at first she didn't know how to react. But she did a complete turnaround. From that day forward, she jumped in and helped out tremendously with the wedding. In fact, my mother became James's biggest fan for the next forty years. I'd sometimes say, "I think you love James more than you love me, because you always take his side when we have a disagreement!"

When James stood up to my mother, she knew that I was leaving the family and going with James and that we were totally committed to each other. We were not going to be pulled apart by someone else's feelings or opinions. In the process of leaving and cleaving, there's no place for arrogance or insensitivity, but strength is a necessary requirement. James showed strength by confronting the issue, and I showed strength by standing with James in what was, for me, an intimidating situation.

His strength and obvious commitment let my mother know that I was going to be okay, that I had a man who was really going to love and take care of me. I trusted my whole heart and soul first to God and then to James.

✦ JAMES

What I remember about that incident with Betty's mom was my recognition of how much Betty truly wanted to leave her parents and cleave to me. That gave me the confidence to do what I did, but I mean to tell you, my knees were knocking! Betty's mom was a powerful lady!

Commitment, in some respects, is like faith: both are only as valid as their object. If, for example, you place your faith in a chair with a broken leg, your faith is only as valid as the chair's ability to support your weight. Regardless of your sincerity, if the chair collapses, it proves that your faith was misplaced and unworthy. The same is true of commitment. If you commit yourself to the wrong things, everything in your life will be undermined.

Where faith and commitment differ is on the importance of *strength*. Pastor Stuart Briscoe tells a story about a man who approached a lake that was frozen over. He was unable to tell how thick the ice was or whether it was sufficient to support his weight, so he began to inch his way across the lake, crawling on his hands and knees and wondering if, at any moment, the ice might give way. When he was about halfway across the lake, still inching his way along, he heard the rumble of an approaching horse and sleigh. A moment later the sleigh thundered past him and continued across the frozen lake to the other side. It was then the man realized the ice was certainly thick enough to support his weight, and he got to his feet, feeling quite foolish.

Here's the point: although the man's faith was weak, the ice was strong, and thus his faith was secure. If, on the other hand, he had charged onto the ice with a tremendously strong faith and the ice had been thin, he would have broken through and drowned—by faith. So even if your faith is shaky, if the object of your faith is strong and dependable, you will be safe and secure. But if your commitment is shaky, your relationship will be shaky and insecure as well.

The strength of your commitment to a worthy object—in this case, your spouse and your marriage—is what will see you through. Having a strong commitment doesn't mean you will never fail, but it means you're serious about persisting and persevering, no matter what else happens—even if your life falls apart.

COMMITMENT IS A COVENANT, NOT A CONTRACT

When we make a commitment, it's important to understand its nature. Perhaps you've heard that marriage is a covenant relationship, not a contractual agreement. What's the difference? In his book *The Blessed Marriage,* our pastor, Robert Morris, gives some excellent examples of the distinction between a *contract* and a *covenant,* which we will summarize here:

- In a contract, you protect your rights and limit your responsibilities. In a covenant, you lay down your rights on behalf of the other person, and you assume responsibilities.
- In a contract, your responsibilities are specified and restricted by the terms of the agreement. In a covenant, all the responsibility is yours.
- A contract may be renegotiated, amended, or broken. A covenant is irrevocable, unconditional, and unbreakable.
- In a covenant relationship, you give up the rights of priority, ownership, and privacy, and you pick up the responsibilities of love, honor, and submission.

- In a contract, if the other party doesn't live up to the agreement, you are freed from your obligation. In a covenant, you agree to lay down your rights and take up all the responsibility—above all, the responsibility to love. No matter what your spouse does, you will keep your covenant commitment. Entering a marriage with a spirit of covenant says, "I give up all my rights in order to meet your needs, even to the point of death. I also assume great responsibility for the success of our marriage."[1]

In our society we are so accustomed to entering contracts that the "no matter what" aspect of a covenant relationship seems daunting. We're tempted to ask, "But what if…" A covenant commitment doesn't look at what-ifs. Instead, it says, "I'm in this for the duration, come what may." The what-ifs may come, and your commitment is certain to be tested, but if you've decided in your heart that you're devoted to your marriage and to your mate, for better or for worse, then you'll have the necessary foundation to withstand the storms of life.

Because Betty and I made a covenant with each other, we've grown together in ways I never imagined possible when we were first married. At the outset my philosophy for marriage was simple: please God and please Betty. That doesn't mean I let her run over me. It simply means that I did what I could—and still do—to care for Betty and to make her feel secure. It means I listen to her concerns, respect her thoughts, and do everything I can to make her feel as if she's a queen married to a king. I want to know what excites her and what interests her, and I want to support her in those areas of her life.

In this way I started looking for opportunities when I could see something sparkle in her eyes—the kind of excitement you see in a mother's face when she talks about her children. I noticed these things and took enjoyment in them. And Betty felt the same way about me. We both found great satisfaction in truly caring about the other person's personal joy and well-being.

The same is as true today as it was fifty years ago. My greatest enjoyment is to see Betty excited. I've learned over the years to glory in her enthusiasm, and she does the same with me. We do things for each other, not out of a sense of duty, but because we legitimately want to do them.

My commitment to Betty comes out even in small ways, such as picking up around the house (if I can beat her to it), making sure the garbage is taken to the curb on time, offering assistance in preparing meals, or noticing a slight change in her hairstyle and telling her how nice she looks. These little things demonstrate a much bigger attitude in my heart: I am committed to Betty, and I honor my commitment out of a sincere, honest desire, not just because I said "I do" in my wedding vows.

I have to tell you that Betty is so efficient at getting things done that she will make the bed as soon as we get up. I recently joked about her efficiency, sharing that when I get up during the night to use the bathroom and come back into the room, she has already made the bed.

✦ BETTY

Never at any time in our marriage have I felt the threat of divorce or the fear that James didn't love me. I did, however, allow the Enemy to suggest such possibilities, but I never believed these ideas were coming from James. Because of the security and safety I have felt with James, I've always known we could work through our challenges.

COMMITMENT MEANS FORSAKING ALL OTHERS

✦ JAMES

Another key part of commitment in marriage is exclusivity. Betty and I are convinced that it's nearly impossible for a couple to maintain their dedication to each other if they have other allegiances. We believe the traditional marriage vow to forsake all others, which is typically understood as simply an admonition against adultery, should extend to *all others,* including parents, friends, and relatives.

We're not suggesting you shut off all contact with the outside world. You still need to maintain relationships with your family and friends, but those relationships cannot be at your spouse's expense. After your commitment to God, your spouse must be your number-one priority. If you want your marriage to thrive, you must leave behind all others and cleave to your mate.

I've seen the power of leaving and cleaving in my marriage to Betty. I knew I had to leave behind not only my old relationships but also my old ways of thinking about myself. I was no longer in charge of my life; I had to consider and treasure my wife's thoughts, feelings, and opinions, and she had to do the same for me. Through the process of leaving and cleaving, we've seen God change us for His purposes, and we've seen Him create a love within us that far surpasses anything we would have dreamed of or accomplished for ourselves.

> *Selfishness is as dangerous to a marriage as other allegiances.*

Soon after Betty and I married, I discovered there was an important person I had to forsake and leave behind in order to cleave to her: *me*. Selfishness is as dangerous to a marriage as other allegiances, and maybe more so, because it's inside the marriage. In the early days I was committed to Betty, but I also wanted to control my schedule and play sports (usually football or basketball), and those things often took first place on my priority list of how I spent my time. But when I focused on myself and lived in a world of self-interest with me, myself, and I as the ultimate pursuit, Betty was squeezed out.

An unhealthy self-focus can show up in marriage in many ways, but the one I've observed most frequently is people trying to shape their spouses according to their own expectations. This is always a mistake. Instead of trying to change your mate, it is best to allow God to shape *you*. He's the only One with the power to bring meaningful change to your life that will stand the test of time and circumstances.

Both you and your spouse came into your marriage as incomplete, flawed people who needed to be changed. In fact, you're still that way, no matter how many years you've been married. We all are. But to expect to see improvement through selfishness or manipulation is foolish. You cannot live for yourself and remain committed to your spouse. And you cannot set your mind to change your spouse. If you do, you're likely to get the kind of change you don't want.

Although both you and your spouse need to be changed, and it may be tempting for you to try to be the agent of change in your spouse's life, God is the only One who can—and *must*—make the changes. If you expect your husband or wife to change you, your trust is misplaced.

Perhaps you're unwilling to change because you don't think it's really necessary. Perhaps you think you have your life all figured out, and you approach your marriage with an attitude that says, "This is just the way I am, and you'll have to learn to live with it—like it or lump it."

If that's your perspective, you're being selfish, and you're well on your way to existing in separate worlds rather than living in love. You must realize that, in so many ways, the strength of your marriage is determined by change—not by your working to change your spouse, but by allowing yourself to be changed through growing experiences, wisdom, insights from others, and the help of your spouse.

In everything, it's always the inside power, which can only come from God, that will bring lasting, transformational change.

COMMITMENT PUSHES US BEYOND FEAR AND FRUSTRATION

✦ BETTY

True commitment also involves stretching. As imperfect people, we get the wrong idea about commitment, and in order to protect ourselves, we commit only so far. Instead of giving everything we have, we hold back, afraid to give ourselves fully because we run the risk of getting hurt. Instead of completely engaging with our mate, we back off and hope to avoid what I call "ugly stuff."

If we'll accept the inevitable challenges of marriage and deal with them in a way that pleases God, understanding full well that everything isn't always going to be roses, then our refusal to back down or give in will deepen and strengthen our commitment and our relationship.

Maybe you intended to build your marriage on the solid ground of a covenant commitment but somehow you started building on something else—whether through ignorance or disobedience, deception or division. Whatever the reason for where you are, God wants you to have a new beginning through a new awareness and a new foundation in Him.

When problems bring disharmony into your relationship, you can easily lose sight of those early days of your marriage and the simple promise you made to always love and cherish each other. The vow to have and to hold fades away in the face of difficulties, so it's up to you to remember the level of commitment you first felt in your relationship and to continue to honor it.

The truth is this: you cannot have a harmonious, God honoring relationship without making a firm, daily decision to honor each other and to stay attuned to each other's thoughts and feelings, no matter what. Otherwise, you won't be living, you'll simply be existing. And you won't even be existing together but rather operating in separate worlds. You may share the same physical space, the same room, but you'll be in different emotional and mental places.

You can come to a place in your relationship where you are strangers, wondering how you ever got along in the first place and unable to recognize or remember the love you once had for each other. It could be compared to the distance you may sense between yourself and God when you don't communicate with Him. Of course, God never leaves us or forsakes us, and that's the level of commitment a husband and wife need to have with each other.

Sadly, over the years James and I have observed many couples living as though they have no common focus or interests. In a way it's as if they are held captive within prison walls they have allowed to be built in their relationship. This is not what God intends! If you are living in this bleak world, you must—with God's help—break free.

When you try to operate in a separate, commitment-free zone, you only do damage to your relationship—possibly far more damage than you realize. A lack of dedication to each other is insidious in the way it begins to harden your heart and your attitudes. If you allow a lack of commitment to creep into your life, you'll find yourself becoming more and more calloused to your spouse's feelings and needs as well as to your own.

BUILDING HEDGES AROUND YOUR COMMITMENT

✦ JAMES

Your commitment will be tested—that's guaranteed—but I don't believe it's wise to intentionally test your commitment. Instead, you should build hedges of protection around your relationship, a buffer zone to keep danger at a distance.

Think of it as you would the foundation of a house. When a homesite is graded, the ground is sloped away from the house so that rainwater will run off and not accumulate next to the foundation. In some regions, particularly where houses have basements, a sump pump is installed beneath the foundation to keep water from accumulating and causing damage. A wise homeowner will have a battery backup for the electric pump in case the power goes out during a storm. The point is that even though a concrete foundation is structurally strong and can bear a lot of weight, it can be undermined over time. Therefore, it's wise to take some simple precautions to protect the foundation from the forces that could cause it to fail.

The same goes for the foundation of commitment in your marriage. Husbands, when you're committed to your wife, you don't put her in a position where she's apt to feel jealous or to wonder if she can trust you. You don't make independent decisions that ought to be made together. Wives, when you're committed to your husband, you don't discuss his weaknesses with your girlfriends. You don't take an issue that you have with your husband to someone else without talking to him first. You don't betray a confidence.

It doesn't matter whether your spouse is naturally trusting or jealous. What matters is your commitment to build hedges and safeguards around your commitment, to shore up the areas where your spouse is weak. These are simple steps. If you want to live in love and have a fulfilling marriage, it only makes sense that you'll do what it takes.

COMMITMENT IS JUST THE BEGINNING

Success in marriage starts with a desire to have the best marriage possible, and it progresses—based on your commitment—to do what it takes to live in love and to have a marriage that thrives.

Your spouse needs to know that you're in the marriage to stay. Commitment is such a bedrock principle for a successful marriage that everything else depends on it. Commitment creates safety, and safety creates a climate in which trust and concern are able to grow.

Without commitment, there's no basis for building trust, teamwork, and unity. But it's a long way from a committed marriage to a thriving marriage. Commitment is absolutely essential, but it's only the foundation, only the beginning. We want to help you take your relationship to the highest level of joy. We don't want you to settle for anything less than the best marriage you can possibly have.

The Old Testament is full of examples of God's commitment and faithfulness to His people. Even when Israel was unfaithful to God, His steadfast commitment remained unshaken. This same commitment to faithfulness is suggested in one of the best-known New Testament passages about marriage: "Husbands, love your wives, just as Christ also loved the church and gave Himself up for her."[2] In the simple phrase "as Christ also loved the church" is found everything about God's commitment and faithfulness to His people. That's the level of commitment needed in a thriving marriage.

"But that's impossible," you say. "No one could replicate the level of commitment that Jesus has for the church." But in the words of Jesus: "Humanly speaking, it is impossible. But not with God. Everything is possible with God."[3] When you come to the end of yourself, that's when you begin to catch a glimpse of God's power and everything that is possible through Him. No, you can't do it on your own. But that's the point. You're not meant to do it on your own.

The transforming power of the Holy Spirit is the same power available to transform and strengthen your marriage, no matter how many times you've failed and no matter how bleak your current situation may seem. "Everything is possible with God."

✦ BETTY

People come to marriage with a commitment to the person they think they see in their spouse. And everyone comes into marriage with a commitment to her or his own self-interests and dreams. James and I want you to understand that the path to your own self-interest lies squarely through the territory of your spouse's best interests and the best interests of your relationship.

If you're looking at your spouse and no longer see what attracted you to him or her in the first place, it's time to stop and reset your lens. Go back in your mind and think, *What were those things that attracted me? Are they just not there?* Were you totally deceived, or might they actually still be there but are hidden? What did you see in your mate that attracted you so magnetically? Is it possible that those things could be rekindled? rediscovered? established more fully? At the same time, are there similar things that could be more fully developed and established in you?

Now, applying the principles of a covenant commitment, are you willing to lay down your rights and take up your responsibility to draw out and develop those possibilities in your mate?

God definitely knew what He was doing when He established covenant commitment as the critical foundation stone for living in love.

 FOR REFLECTION AND DISCUSSION

What are the basic differences between a contract and a covenant?

What qualities attracted you to your spouse early in your relationship? Do you still see them?

In what ways is commitment a challenge in your marriage?

Are you and your spouse existing in two different worlds? (Remember, Jesus came that you might have life and to set the captives free.[4])

5

Building Trust

Integrity over time brings confidence

in the other's character.

JAMES

*L*ife isn't always easy, and neither are relationships. You will encounter times when your dedication—both to God and to your spouse—will be challenged. How should you respond? What should you do in order to honor the commitments you've made? Those are the times when you most need to trust each other.

Trust is built on the foundation of commitment—first, and ultimately, to God and then to each other. Trust helps to guide us when we are uncertain about any number of actions or reactions. For example, it's extremely difficult for men and women to understand how the other feels. God created men and women with different strengths, weaknesses, and desires, which we need to understand in order to move forward in building trust and commitment.

Personally, I don't think you can lump men or women into a single trait or category, saying, "Men are always like this, and women are always like that." Every person is unique in so many ways, regardless of gender. I will admit, though, that it's fair to say most men are visual in the way they process the world around them. They are able to compartmentalize their lives and deal with indi-

> *Trust is built on the foundation of commitment—first, and ultimately, to God and then to each other.*

vidual crises as they crop up. Women are often more emotionally sensitive and tend to homogenize the crises in their lives. It's important that we understand these differences so we can honor them in each other and, in so doing, establish trust.

I understand that God created Betty the way He did. She pays closer attention to her emotions than I do, especially when it comes to feelings of security. She wants to know that I consider her and hold her in high regard. When I honor her, I build up trust. If I don't honor her feelings and even work against them by talking down to her or telling her she just needs to toughen up and deal with something, I succeed only in tearing down her trust and disrupting her peace of mind.

And it works both ways: I trust her and depend on her just as much. In this, we have great peace and stability in our relationship. We both know that the other person has our best interests at heart.

Betty and I have worked long and hard to learn more and more about each other so that we can always consider each other. Whatever Betty considers important, I consider important. Whatever I feel is necessary, Betty feels is necessary. We don't always understand why those things are important or necessary, but it doesn't matter. We just know that if the other person deems something to be important, we need to make it a priority for ourselves as well.

This type of thinking is the cornerstone of trust between a husband and wife, but it doesn't stop there. It's also an important way of thinking about your relationship—as a team. You're on the same team, and you need to act like it.

God said He made us to "be one," not only with Him, but with each other (see John 17:20–24). Becoming one with God, as Jesus said, is the only way we can live in harmony and love with one another. Unity between ourselves in our marriages and with other people in the body of Christ comes from our oneness with God.

TRUST TAKES TIME

As important as trust is in a marriage, it doesn't happen right away. Trust is a bridge that must be built, brick by brick, between you and your spouse. When Betty and I were first married, we trusted our commitment to each other, but we honestly didn't know each other well enough to fully identify the other's strengths and weaknesses. This initially made it difficult for us to trust each other as fully as we needed to in order for our relationship to develop in a healthy way.

✦ BETTY

Yes, building trust has taken time and a lot of practice. Often, in order to put trust into action, we have to find a balance between what I want and what James wants. We have to love and respect each other enough that we don't step on each other's gifts. In the case of our relationship, James is an extrovert who absolutely loves being around other people who have needs, and he loves ministering to them. James feels that if he's not helping someone, or at least trying to, he's not living fully. I like people too, but I also need to have some space, because I'm an introvert, and extensive interactions with lots of people wear me down. The very thing that energizes James drains me.

We've been able to understand and appreciate this about each other over the years, and we have built up trust in each other to respect our feelings and find appropriate compromises. I will go with James to be around a lot of people and meet that particular need of his, and he will try to leave early with me so I can enjoy my quiet time alone or just with him.

✦ JAMES

It took quite a while to figure out our differences! Looking back with the benefit of fifty years of perspective, I can see how limited our understanding was of the other's personality and how we had to build our trust—and our trustworthiness—gradually over time.

For example, I've always been athletic, and I especially enjoyed playing basketball. I loved to shoot hoops with my friends. From before we were married to many years afterward, I spent a lot of time with a basketball in my hands just having fun with my friends and working on my skills. (Golf later took the place of basketball as a sometimes foolish commitment to my own selfish interests.)

One day early in our marriage, I told Betty I was heading out to the gym to play basketball with my friends.

"I don't want you to go," she said.

"Do you have something else you want to do?" I asked.

"No, not really. I just want you to stay here." Betty didn't want me to leave because she wanted my time and attention. Suddenly we had an opportunity to build some trust between us. This incident could easily have challenged my commitment. I could have looked at Betty's request as a control issue, as if she didn't trust me to be away and have fun with my friends. Betty could have looked at my desire to be with my friends as not being responsive to her needs, as an attempt to get away from her for a while.

Betty wasn't consciously trying to test my commitment to her, but she was giving me an opportunity to decide which was more important to me—her desires or my self-interests. I didn't always make the right decision, but over time I began to learn what was truly important. It wasn't that Betty felt she had to keep an eye on me; she just didn't want to be apart. And it wasn't that I was trying to hurry out of the house to get a breather from her; I just wanted to do something I considered fun.

When this confrontation occurred, we needed to learn how to adjust our time and ways to our new life as a couple. We had to learn how to respond and not react, how not to judge the other's actions but to look at the other person's heart. When I ignored her wishes and did my own thing, Betty cried because she felt all alone. The fact is, I was being a jerk. We knew we loved each other, but we needed to grow in our understanding of each other's needs.

We thank God that we openly talked through these issues. In reality, the issue was far more than her needing to learn to trust me. I had every bit as much to learn about considering her needs and desires and assuring her that she was and always would be first in my heart.

TRUST IS EARNED

Betty and I established mutual trust based on what we observed about each other, but I know there were times when my actions might have made me appear untrustworthy. Trust always has to be earned. But if you fail or disappoint your spouse, what is the necessary ingredient to give the other person hope? I think it is your spouse's ability to discern the sincerity and intention of your heart.

This isn't something we can talk other people into; they have to see it for themselves over time.

Trust always has to be earned.

Once your heart is known, it can provide a buffer for whatever failures or frailties or disappointing actions might otherwise undermine your spouse's trust in you.

Because Betty could see the depths of my heart and soul—that I wanted more than anything else to please God and to correct those things in my life that might not please Him or might disappoint her—she was able to continue to trust me even when my actions didn't align with my intentions.

✦ BETTY

I agree that, when it comes to trust, nothing is more important to keep in mind than intentions. It is easy to lose trust when your spouse says or does something that offends or disappoints you. But when these things happen, it's always good to pause, take a deep breath, and take inventory of his or her intentions.

As James mentioned, he and I have learned to trust each other's heart, not just each other's actions. Of course we try to make our actions consistent with our intentions and to keep our words trustworthy and true. At times, though, even to this day, we disappoint each other. Then we have to look past the words and actions and focus on intentions.

For instance, when James goes to the pantry to retrieve something I need, I may call to him and ask for another item. If he doesn't hear my exact request, he's likely to raise his voice and say, "What?" This tends to cause me to raise my voice and repeat myself, and this raising of our voices can result in irritation or even a heated discussion. When that happens, we seek to go back to trusting the intent of each other's heart.

When James raised his voice to ask for clarification on what I needed, he wasn't yelling at me; he was trying to be heard from another room. When I raised my voice in response, I wasn't yelling at him; I was trying to make sure he understood my request, because his hearing has diminished as he's gotten older. In situations like this, James has said that he feels as if I'm snapping at him or being impatient. From my perspective, however, I'm simply trying to make sure he heard and understood what I have said.

✦ JAMES

I promise not to do this too often, but I want to share another story.

✦ BETTY

Okay, if you insist.

✦ JAMES

There was a husband who believed his wife might be hard of hearing. So he asked his doctor, "What should I do to find out for sure if she's had any hearing loss?"

"Try this," the doctor replied. "When you're at home, if she's facing away from you, from a distance of about thirty feet, say in a normal voice, 'What's for dinner?' If she doesn't answer you, move a few feet closer and again say, 'What's for dinner?' The longer it takes for her to answer, the more likely she has a hearing problem."

The husband went home and tried the experiment as soon as he walked through the door. His wife was in the kitchen. He shouted from far away, "What's for dinner?" and received no reply. So he moved closer and asked the question again. He did this several more times until he was standing right behind his wife, asking again, "What's for dinner?"

"For the fifth time," she said, turning to look at him, "the answer is chicken!"

So who had the problem hearing?

✦ BETTY

Actually, that sounds a bit familiar, doesn't it, James?

Getting back to my point about trust... The intentions of our heart are usually in the right place even if our words and our tone of voice don't seem to show it. We would never purposely try to hurt or insult each other, so we're able to move forward by trusting each other's intent. And of course we can do that because we've built up trust in each other over time.

That's what trust is: using your words and actions to build security for your spouse and feeling as if your spouse always has your best interest at heart. When those words and actions don't line up with what you hope for, trust means you still believe the good intentions are there.

Jimmy Draper, former president of the Southern Baptist Sunday School Board and our pastor at the time, once said from the pulpit, "If either my wife or I hear something our spouse says that hurts us, we know we misunderstood what was said, because neither of us would ever intentionally hurt the other person." This inspired James and me to know the same thing in our relationship.

TRUSTING THROUGH TRIALS

✦ JAMES

Our mutual trust was really put to the test when I began to travel extensively in my evangelism ministry. Betty would occasionally come along, but I was often on the road more than 250 days a year, and once we had kids, she wasn't as free to travel. Not only were we apart during those times, but Betty knew that many people were drawn to me in my ministry—including a number of attractive women. This was a problem for Betty, but because of her shyness and insecurity and her unwarranted feelings of not being pretty, smart, or talented enough, she would clam up and not tell me how she felt.

I knew she was struggling, because when I called home from the road every day, she would tell me how lonely she was without me there. But when I was home, she would act depressed and not want to go anywhere or do anything. When she wouldn't accept any invitations where she might have to share me, I told her I thought she was being unreasonably possessive.

The only way I knew to confront the problem was to tackle it head-on, but that made Betty feel more vulnerable and added to her fear that she wasn't living up to my expectations. When matters would come to a head, I often would have to leave the house and drive around to cool off, pray, and get some perspective. Betty's response was to storm into our bedroom and slam the door. We eventually learned how to deal with our disagreements and misunderstandings more constructively, but for a time we struggled and merely coped with our differences.

What tipped the balance, I think, in the direction of growth and progress was that, through the process of resolving our disagreements and getting to the root of our misunderstandings, we learned that we truly had each other's best interests at heart. We concluded that we could trust each other to always work toward resolution and reconciliation. Later in our marriage when I reached a point of burnout in my ministry and began to spiral downward emotionally, physically, and spiritually, that foundation of trust became the glue that held our commitment together.

Eventually all these trials and tests became bricks in a rock-solid bridge of trust between us.

THE SECURITY OF TRUST

Security is important in any commitment, because it lets both spouses know that their dedication is solid and that they can feel safe in devoting themselves to each other. Trust and security go hand in hand.

I have learned to trust Betty's indescribable watchful care with children. When our daughter Rhonda was young, she had asthma, which would cause periodic choking episodes. When these occurred, Rhonda would sometimes panic, and so would I. But Betty would step in and handle the situation with grace and skill. It was amazing to observe her incredible calm and control whenever there was an emergency with the children. I never had to worry that she would be distracted from caring for them or that she would lose sight of her other responsibilities. This provided great security for me when I was on the road. While I was off helping other people, I knew she had the home front covered.

I also have come to trust Betty completely with our finances. (And she trusts me to make sure the money is there!) But early in our marriage, Betty wouldn't even write a check for anything because she was afraid she would make a mistake with our finances. She lacked confidence in all the great, hidden abilities God had entrusted to her. Today, however, Betty manages our entire budget, paying every bill, writing every check, and maintaining our records perfectly—all with unshakable confidence.

TRUST OUTSIDE THE COMFORT ZONE

✦ BETTY

I appreciate how James has supported me as I've learned how to take on new challenges. Knowing you can trust your husband definitely helps when you have to step outside your comfort zone. That's not easy for me because I've always been more comfortable keeping with my routine; I like sticking with things the way I know them as a wife, mother, grandmother, and homemaker. So when James invited me to start cohosting *Life Today* with him, I was very uncomfortable. I would never have dreamed of a role like that for myself; it's miles outside my comfort zone.

I have a tendency to withdraw into my shell, but through our mutual trust, James helped me open up as we began to host the program together. The more we prepared to start the show, the more I trusted that James would help me through it. The fact is, I not only lean on God, but I also lean on James, and both always lift me up and build me up.

I still recall the day when God sealed the deal. He spoke plainly to my heart about the show, telling me I needed to get outside my comfort zone in order to give of myself. As I've moved forward in obedience and trust, I've not only become more comfortable with hosting the show, but I've also repeatedly come away from tapings more blessed as I let God use me for His glory and His kingdom purposes.

BUILDING ON TRUST

✦ JAMES

If commitment is the solid foundation in a relationship, trust is the glue that holds everything together. If trust is strong, it can supply the measure of grace necessary to secure a marriage in the storms of life. Trust expects the best and thinks the best of the other person. Trust looks beyond words and actions and sees the intentions of the heart. That's crucial when a spouse's words and actions might be called into question.

I have a natural, legitimate desire to care for people with needs. In particular, I have a soft spot for women, not just because I believe they are beautiful, but also because I see their vulnerability. If Betty and I lacked mutual trust, this sensitivity to women in distress could have destroyed our marriage.

Growing up, I saw my mother get hurt time and again, and I often saw her alone and lonely. My mother was a very sweet woman who made a lot of mistakes in life and didn't receive much love. Witnessing her suffering created a sensitivity in me and a strong desire to help anyone in need. Those are positive traits, but in the wrong circumstances they can also be negative. Strength, sensitivity, and caring are what most women are looking for in a relationship—more than physical or sexual attraction. As my evangelism ministry began to grow, some women were drawn to my strength, confidence, and compassion, and this made me vulnerable to compromise. Believe me, I understand those things, and it could have destroyed my life—except for the grace of God and the trust of a committed, loving wife.

I had to learn that any genuine love or compassion on my part to try to help women with needs was actually not going to help them. It only put both them and me at risk. I had to point them to somebody else or to some other form of encouragement or counsel, because otherwise we could have easily developed an unhealthy "soul connection." That kind of compatibility and dependence can become very dangerous and damaging because it fills a legitimate need in an inappropriate way. A man and woman can begin to feed their personal desires or longings simply by spending time talking together. But neither one is getting better for it. I think that's what has happened in a lot of churches and ministries when pastors and leaders get caught up in wrongful relationships.

It's important to point out that the closer we are to God and the more legitimate our relationship is with Him, the more attractive we can become to other people. Betty is so sweet, loving, and fun that it would be easy for another man to be drawn to her. If she didn't have a husband who really loved her and with whom she was happy, we could have a serious problem. The same goes for me. If I were unhappy with Betty and found that someone else was attracted to me, any number of negative consequences could occur.

True love is something that grows throughout the years.

TRUSTING GOD IS THE KEY

✦ BETTY

As I look back on my life, I see that my love for James has become so much more than the initial physical attraction I felt when I met him. We have a genuine spiritual relationship. He and I have learned to love each other through God's love, and trust is a major expression of this type of love.

Trust in a marriage relationship is like knowing and loving God. You grow through knowledge of His Word and the things He does in your life, even in challenging situations. You learn, change, grow, and develop. At the moment we got married, James and I couldn't possibly have known the fullness of our love. There was so much to learn! We had to trust God and understand that the more love we gave to each other, the more God would release through us. That is the ultimate trust: first in God, and then in each other.

I've also learned to trust God in the area of living in love. True love is something that grows throughout the years. I love James more today than when we walked down the aisle. Back then, I was just beginning to see glimpses of why I loved him. But even in those glimpses, I trusted that our love would grow and would never diminish. I have given James my love continually for the past fifty years, and I have more of it now than I had when we started.

✦ JAMES

As Betty and I were discussing this chapter, she reminded me of the old Smith Barney ads in which their spokesman, actor John Houseman, would say, "We make money the old-fashioned way. We earn it." "To be honest," Betty said, "trust has to be earned the old-fashioned way as well. It's hard work!"

How badly do you want it? There is a price to pay. Building trust requires love, devotion, respect, sacrifice, desire, and forgiveness. To me, this is what trust is all about. It can't be achieved without determination.

 FOR REFLECTION AND DISCUSSION

In your experience, what builds trust in a relationship? What destroys trust?

What changes might you make that would help build trust in your marriage?

6

Baggage: The Junk in the Trunk

Junk can be found in everyone's past.

BETTY

As a young girl, I dreamed, as I believe most girls do, that I would marry a knight in shining armor who would sweep me off my feet, and we would have the perfect life together. Everything would just be heavenly. We would get along beautifully, always agree on everything, never argue, and have ideal children who always obeyed and never rebelled.

When I met and married James, I got my knight, but that's where the fantasy ended. I didn't realize that, like every couple, we had personality differences and baggage from the past that would affect our marriage.

Your baggage is the sum total of your life experiences, good and bad. It includes personality traits, ways of thinking, emotional states, habits, hang-ups, feelings about yourself, personal preferences, vices. You can dress up your baggage or disguise it, but somehow, someway, sometime it's going to be exposed.

And if you're not prepared to deal with it—or if you don't deal with it—you're going to be in big trouble.

James was very up-front about his baggage, and he had plenty. Because of his upbringing, he could lose his temper, and he had a determined, almost desperate independence. Because he was used to doing everything on his own, whenever I would question his decisions, he easily answered, "Don't tell me I can't..." and "Don't get in my way." He also battled lust, which was rooted in things he had observed while growing up in a degraded environment.

These things hurt me because they touched on a few suitcases of my own, such as feelings of inadequacy and low self-worth, which I wanted to keep closed

> *Your baggage is the sum total of your life experiences, good and bad.*

and put away. In fact, I tried to pretend my baggage didn't exist. I wanted to hide it or disguise it, hoping it would disappear. But in a marriage, no matter how much you want to hide your baggage, it will eventually appear. Even if you try to keep it out of sight and out of mind, inevitably you or your spouse will trip over it, and someone may get hurt.

We've devoted a whole section of this book to talking about commitment, because a firm, unshakable commitment to each other is absolutely necessary in order to deal with very real issues. If you don't have a rock-solid commitment and devotion to your spouse, the weight of your baggage will strain your relationship, possibly even to the breaking point.

Because James and I married fairly young, when I came into the marriage, I didn't recognize that I was also bringing junk in my baggage. I knew I wanted a husband to give me security, to love me, and to be devoted to me, but I didn't see those desires as a potential problem that I was carrying into the relationship. Sometimes we have the wrong idea of what devotion to a spouse means. I knew I wanted James to love God—which he did—but I think I also wanted all his attention. I was looking for my identity, which I felt I had never really found in my life, and I brought a lot of fear and insecurity along with low self-esteem.

Having never quite measured up—at least in my own mind—to my mother's expectations, I harbored a fear that I wouldn't measure up to James's expectations either. That fear may have been rooted in my early childhood, perhaps because of some of my health issues. I was sick a lot as a baby and a small child, and I had asthma. I remember the fear of not being able to breathe.

Mostly, I didn't know who the real Betty was. I didn't see myself as athletic like my brother or smart like my sister, so I think I put all my hopes and dreams—and my search for who I was—into my marriage relationship. I thought I could have everything I wanted and needed from my marriage—security, purpose, fulfillment—and that it would all happen naturally. Well, it didn't. It wasn't James's responsibility to bring all this to me, but I didn't understand that.

So I would be disappointed if he wanted to play ball with the guys or do other things. I felt it meant he didn't really want to spend time with me. He would tell me he loved me and everything, but I wanted all his attention. When it didn't happen, my disappointment rose, and then jealousy seeped in. I was so insecure and felt as if people were robbing me by taking James's time and attention away from me.

Of course I didn't want anybody to know I was unhappy, so I focused on trying to be the perfect Christian wife and mother and on doing everything right. I now had several more suitcases in my baggage set—insecurity, disappointment, jealousy, and pride—but I was hiding all of them in my heart. I was about to explode, and I didn't know what to do! Having grown up in a Baptist church, I had the idea that if you didn't bother the devil, he wouldn't bother you. I didn't know he was playing on all these tender places in my heart, twisting them around and making them larger than life. All I knew was that I was miserable, and I didn't know how to express myself to James. And I surely didn't know how to overcome my problems. I didn't recognize any of this when we were first married, but when you live with someone day after day, eventually things start to come out and need to be dealt with.

THE POWER OF FORGIVENESS

✦ JAMES

When it came to dealing with my painful childhood, I started by ignoring it. I had no desire to go back to that time of my life or to work through any of those feelings or even to allow God to restore that part of my life. I didn't want to think about it, let alone talk about it. But then my friend Billy Foote told me that, not only did I need to deal with it, but I also needed to tell my story to others, to share my pain, and to see how much it helped other people. I took his advice and discovered something interesting: opening up to others about my pain and hurt helped bring healing to me.

My father was a drunk who stole from his family, abandoned us, tried to kill my mother, and then threatened my life. Naturally, I had a lot of pain and bitterness. My father never did anything for me except bring heartache and trouble. And yet, as I began to open up this area of my life to God, He gave me a genuine love for my father, a man I never really knew.

As I forgave my father, God brought restoration to my heart to the point where I surprised myself in the way I dealt with my dad. I distinctly remember a time that I found him passed out from drunkenness and covered in his own vomit. I knelt down, put my arms around his filthy, smelly body, and said, "I don't know you, but I love you." And I meant it.

When I held on to my pain and bitterness, I was being held captive by someone else's wrongs.

That level of forgiveness was possible only because of God's grace. The Lord gave me the ability to forgive this man who had caused me so much pain. God makes miracles out of our biggest mistakes and our greatest weaknesses.

When I began to deal with my hurts, I realized something crucial about them: when I held on to my pain and bitterness, I was being held captive by someone else's wrongs. But when I made a clear determination to forgive my father, I was released from my captivity to bitterness and anger about his addiction and his treatment of my mother and me.

Again, this forgiveness was possible only by the grace of God, but it's available to everyone. If you receive the grace of God, you'll release it to others. If you don't release it, you haven't really received it.

Forgiveness is guaranteed to heal you, and it will enhance the healing process in others. I can say this with the utmost authority, because I've seen it at work in my own life and marriage. When other people wrong you, what they do with the situation is their issue. But when you forgive them, you get well. You get better. To fail to forgive is to invite a form of bondage along with recurring defeat and misery.

We have an innate desire to rise up against injustice, but when we take vengeance against those who have wronged us, we're putting ourselves in God's place. God said that vengeance is His. If you harshly judge others, it will come back on your own head. An attitude of bitterness, judgment, and revenge never pays. "See to it that no one comes short of the grace of God; that no root of bitterness springing up causes trouble, and by it many be defiled" (Hebrews 12:15, NASB).

Instead, you need to forgive. Forgiveness doesn't let other people off the hook for what they've done, but it lets you off the hook for what they've done. That is the mystery of forgiveness. Forgiveness doesn't mean there won't be consequences, even painful ones. It does mean that you are set free from trying to exact your own consequences.

Hunger and hurt: everyone brings a measure of both to a marriage. But you don't have to settle for living your life hungry and hurt. Forgiveness heals. Forgiveness frees.

WHEN THE TABLES ARE TURNED

What if you're the one in need of forgiveness? What if you've done things in the past that you regret but can't undo? If you're looking at your marriage and feeling that you've messed up so badly that things can never be put right, allow us to inject a bit of hope into your heart.

In the story of the woman at the well,[1] when Jesus began to talk with her, their conversation revealed that she had been married five times and was living with yet another man. In other words, she had messed up time and time again. But Jesus did not condemn her or take her to task for her past. He offered her forgiveness and a chance to start anew.

Likewise, in the story of the woman caught in the act of adultery, Jesus didn't condemn the woman for her sin; He gave her a fresh start.[2] So no matter where you've been or where you are today in your marriage, God offers you forgiveness and a fresh start. All He asks is that you come to the source.[3]

MOVING FORWARD

One certainty about the past is that it can't be changed. What's done is done. However, that doesn't mean it can never be forgiven, restored, or redeemed. I've seen too many turnarounds and heard too many stories of reconciliation to believe that a couple's situation is truly irreconcilable if both parties are willing to submit themselves to God. Regardless of whether the failures, disappointments, and challenges in your marriage are holdovers from the past or are a present reality, you can't let those failures and disappointments stick around.

If you want to live in love with your mate, you can't be held captive by past pain or present problems, and you can't live your life in denial. Some people appear capable of blocking out their problems, and both spouses will tell you they have no major issues in their marriage. But if you look closer, you'll typically find that they've accommodated themselves to a kind of low-grade mutual discontent. True forgiveness and restoration are so much better than settling for less than the best in your marriage.

Betty and I encourage each other to be the best we can be. But how could Betty speak to me about my compulsiveness, my lack of discipline, or my potential addiction to sweets if she didn't believe that I truly desire to submit myself to God?

For Betty, seeing my desire to submit myself to God and to put the past behind me causes her to trust me more. She does this, not because I never fail, but because in my failure I not only want to get up, but I want her to help me get up. And it's the same with her. When she falls down, I don't put her down. I pick her up.

If you and your spouse have carried a lot of negative baggage into your marriage, you may find it takes divine intervention to help you realize that you've truly been forgiven and that forgiveness means your sins have been covered and blotted out. Forgiveness doesn't mean that every bad thing has been blotted from your memory, but it does mean that the blood of Christ covers everything. And if you're willing to offer grace to the person who has failed you, you'll often find that, in return, you receive the same measure of grace to overcome your disappointment and hurt. That's when having a relationship with God can really make a difference in a couple's relationship.

When we are willing to admit, "This really does hurt, and I can't seem to forgive, and I sure can't seem to forget," when we feel as if grace and forgiveness are beyond our reach, that's when we recognize our need for God. Just as we all need grace in order to be forgiven, we likewise need grace to forgive others, to deal with the painful aspects, and to anticipate improvement and growth as we move forward.

GETTING TO HONESTY

Ideally, a couple will have made amends with the past before they get married, during the time they're dating and deciding whether to make a lifelong commitment to each other. Ideally, every marriage would be founded on open and honest communication and no secrets. We understand, however, that most marriages don't start out that way. There's almost always some hidden baggage.

Although I wasn't eager to think about my past, much less talk about it, I didn't keep any secrets from Betty, and she didn't keep any secrets from me. Nevertheless, as time went on and we encountered various circumstances in our marriage, we had to remain committed to open and honest communication in order for it to happen.

I believe a marriage relationship should be so precious, with such a depth of commitment, that you could share with your spouse your innermost heart feelings, battles, struggles, concerns, challenges, and failures. I don't believe every couple has reached that point, and some are nowhere close. And I don't believe that, because of reading this book, you should suddenly start blurting out all your issues, failures, thoughts, and practices. Still, this is a worthy goal, and by the power of the Holy Spirit, who offers grace and forgiveness, every couple can achieve a high level of transparency and honesty.

I am convinced that God's design is for your marriage relationship to be strong enough and your commitment to God to be strong enough that you could say to your spouse, "I've failed," and both of you can bear up. If husbands and wives hold back things from each other, the marriage will not be as healthy as it could and should be. My relationship with Betty is best when I can honestly tell her that I'm having thoughts or desires that are very disturbing to me and that I want her to pray with me about it, without her thinking, *There must really be something wrong with you.* Without that freedom I would be afraid to acknowledge that I'm battling something, and that fear would make me much more susceptible to defeat and failure. But if I can be open and honest with Betty, and if she can come alongside me with compassion and care and pray with me, I'm confident I can have victory in every area of my life. As we'll discuss in more depth in chapter 10, being honest about our struggles and temptations weakens their hold on us and allows us to learn how to walk in freedom.

I can tell you that Betty and I are truly that close. And we believe you can be that close with your spouse as well. We're close enough that if we had something between us, we would be able to talk about who we should approach to help us resolve the issue. I wouldn't go running off to my friends to talk about

Betty, and she wouldn't go running off to her friends to talk about me. We trust each other enough that we're going to talk to each other first about the issue and then get outside help if it's needed to solve the disagreement.

What if one spouse won't talk? In that case, where does the other spouse go for help? Oftentimes one spouse feels betrayed, or maybe the relationship has become abusive, in which case the threatened spouse needs to find outside help. Whenever the issues that divide you seem larger than the two of you can handle together, you're wise to seek another couple or a counselor who can mediate and bring an objective perspective. If possible, go for help together. If not, go alone. Whatever you do, choose a wise counselor who will impart biblical truth and who will come alongside your marriage with love and compassion. Don't look for help in inappropriate relationships or in situations that will only turn to gossip.

A WORD TO THE UNCONVINCED

If you're still determined to stay closed off, I hope you can see that Betty and I have nothing but compassion and concern for your well-being. Please understand that you're keeping a potentially volatile container under unnecessary pressure, and you're risking an explosion. If you simply will not face your issues and concerns, it's difficult for me to recommend that you throw counseling into the mix. Sometimes when I'm counseling a couple, one will say, "I'm not going to change. I'm not going to do this, and I'm not going to do that. I'm just going to hang in there and let the rough end drag and keep a stiff upper lip." All I can say is that's a miserable way to live. And it doesn't have to be that way.

If your spouse is taking this hard line, the best thing you can do is pray. Trust the conviction brought by the Holy Spirit and the beauty of God's love to get the prodigal out of the pigpen and to help him or her realize that life at home is so much better with a fully restored relationship. No matter what you've done, where you've been, or how you've failed, your life today can be so much better. Keep in mind that God can create a masterpiece from the pieces of a broken-up life.

FOR REFLECTION AND DISCUSSION

What baggage—yours and your spouse's—showed up early in your marriage?

For what issues has it been difficult for you to forgive your spouse? Over what issues has your spouse struggled to forgive you?

In what areas do you want to extend grace to your husband or wife?

7

Broken Commitments

Failure is not final.

JAMES

ooking back at my early years of marriage, I can see how foolish I was in a lot of areas. I was too self-absorbed, and I easily could have been a "my way or the highway" jerk. I was very impatient, and to this day, even in my sixties, I acknowledge that any manifestation of patience on my part has to be from God's enabling Spirit.

I was also too competitive, and this spirit carried over even into my ministry. Seeing records set for attendance and responses became, on occasion, far too important to me. I thank God that I recognized these damaging traits and began to deal with them prayerfully. And praise God that Betty was the opposite of me—unselfish and patient, especially with me.

One of my greatest regrets is that I let the success of my ministry get in the way of my success as a husband and father. For many years when my kids were young and even into high school, I traveled too much and was away from home up to 80 percent of the time. This created undue pressure on my marriage and forced Betty to draw heavily on her commitment to God and to me.

I was committed to Betty, but I also was committed to the ministry I felt God had called me to, and travel was part of accomplishing the mission. The truth is that I was so busy trying to do the work of the Lord that I was actually living outside of God's will.

It is difficult to pinpoint the timetable, but after ten or fifteen years of preaching in citywide crusades, I was reading the Bible to get ideas for sermons rather than to discover life for myself. I neglected normal prayer times with my ministry team, and if I prayed before I walked to the pulpit each night, it was usually to beg God to help me even though I knew I had neglected much-needed time with Him. I was battling the problems of lust and too much interest in golf and other outdoor pursuits and was trying to escape the pressure and responsibility of speaking many times a day. In short, I had lost my intimate relationship with God, and that lack had spilled over into a loss of intimacy with my wife and family.

This was a mistake, but God made a miracle out of it when Betty finally called me on it. She could have questioned my commitment to her, but fortunately she didn't. Instead, she lovingly expressed concern for my lack of joy and peace and for my self-centeredness. She prayed continually for me to find freedom and rest in Christ. I resisted or neglected the counsel of several friends who were trying to get me the help I needed, and things only worsened. When I reached the end of myself, I finally recognized and admitted my weaknesses. In brokenness I confessed both to Betty and to our children that I had failed in my commitment to them.

After I finally admitted I had a problem I couldn't face on my own, I submitted myself to godly counsel and prayer. Through Betty's prayers and the help of caring friends, I experienced miraculous, supernatural deliverance and renewal. God used the prayers of a humble Christian brother, a carpet cleaner by trade, to release me from the power of the tormenting spirits of anger, lust, and pride that were oppressing my life. When I lifted my voice to God out of the horrible pit I had dug for myself, He not only inclined His ear to hear my cry, but in mercy He also reached down and picked me up.

And He can do the same for you. "But, James, you have no idea what I've done or what I'm facing." You're right. Yet I have seen God rescue and redeem both individuals and couples from the deepest, darkest pits imaginable, whether those were pits of their own making or pits dug by their beloved spouses.

Your issue may be lust, greed, anger, infidelity, pornography, or substance abuse. Or maybe it's low self-esteem, insecurity, compulsive eating or spending, jealousy, or an unhealthy emotional attachment to someone other than your spouse. Whatever is seeking to tear down your marriage and undermine your commitment to your mate, you need to know that God is bigger than that circumstance or sin. If you will humbly turn to Him and anchor yourself in His unfailing commitment to you and your spouse, you will find that God is in your midst, a victorious warrior who is mighty to save.[1] No pit is too deep or too dark that God cannot rescue you from it, if you're willing.[2]

With the clarity of hindsight, I can now see how the Enemy was trying to undermine my life, marriage, and ministry by tempting me to do God's work apart from God's will. Like many successful ministers, I had become far too much the visible centerpiece of my ministry, and everything revolved around me. When God brought me to the breaking point and I surrendered myself to Him, everything changed. Not only was my marriage to Betty strengthened and our chil-

> *No pit is too deep or too dark that God cannot rescue you from it, if you're willing.*

dren positively affected, but the entire ministry was completely redirected. God led me to remove my name from the ministry. The James Robison Evangelistic Association became Life Outreach International. We were no longer personality centered but purpose centered in every respect.

Betty and I are living examples of this fact: both ministries and marriages have serious difficulties, but God provides a way for every couple to overcome any challenge. The battles we face will never go away, but we do not have to live in defeat.

BROKEN COMMITMENTS AND GOD'S WORD

✦ BETTY

James and I can speak with authority on broken commitments because we have seen over and over again in our lives and in the lives of those we know how God can restore people after they've broken commitments and made terrible mistakes.

One of the best-known examples of restoration in the Bible is the story of David and Bathsheba. David is considered the greatest king in Israel's history, but he ascended to the throne from humble beginnings as a shepherd boy. Referred to by the prophet Samuel as a man after God's own heart, David was used mightily by God to defeat Goliath, the most looming threat to Israel's safety and security, and to face down Israel's greatest enemies.[3]

Once on the throne, however, David began to make mistake after mistake. Perhaps the worst was when he lusted after the beautiful Bathsheba, committed adultery with her, and then, after she became pregnant, arranged the death of her husband. It's difficult to imagine a greater breach of integrity and commitment than that.

Bathsheba's husband, Uriah, on the other hand, is a shining example of keeping commitments and living with integrity. When David called him home from the battlefield, hoping to create a plausible cover-up for Bathsheba's pregnancy by giving her husband leave to be with her for a few days, Uriah refused to violate his commitments. Instead, he said, "The Ark and the armies of Israel and Judah are living in tents, and…my master's men are camping in the open fields. How could I go home to wine and dine and sleep with my wife? I swear that I would never do such a thing."[4]

Of course, Uriah's integrity cost him his life, which illustrates a sobering truth about broken commitments: they have consequences, and often those consequences affect innocent people—spouses, children, family, friends—who may have had nothing to do with the broken commitment. Sometimes the consequence of a broken commitment is divorce, especially when one spouse is not willing to make a change.

In the case of David and Bathsheba, not only was Uriah killed as a consequence of their actions, but Bathsheba's child also died shortly after birth.[5] Yet amid the consequences, the suffering, and the pain, God was able to bring redemption and restoration. He later gave David and Bathsheba another child, Solomon, who succeeded David on the throne of Israel and became known as the wisest man who ever lived.[6] Although David had made a terrible decision that damaged the lives of many people, when he genuinely repented of his sin and sought restoration and forgiveness, God restored him and used him mightily to share great truths through his life and the psalms that he wrote.

Another example of the restoration of a broken commitment is the story of Simon Peter, one of Jesus's closest disciples. When Jesus was falsely accused by the people who had authorized His arrest, Peter denied his association with Jesus in three distinct encounters. Just hours before, Peter had been a staunch defender of Jesus, even to the point of drawing a sword in the Garden of Gethsemane and slashing off the ear of one of the men who had come to arrest Jesus.[7] But under pressure, Peter broke his commitment to Jesus, denying that he even knew Him.

Peter was definitely faint of heart in that dark hour, but Jesus gave him another chance. After Jesus's death and resurrection, He appeared once again to His disciples and specifically to Peter.[8] In this encounter Peter's denials were forgiven, and he was restored to the point that he became the keynote speaker at Pentecost.[9]

These stories from the Bible are just two of the many glorious illustrations of God's redemptive desires. James and I have seen countless other examples ourselves. For instance, over the past two years, we have been privileged to get to know Josh and Katie Hamilton. If you're a baseball fan, you've probably heard Josh's story.

In 1999 he was drafted number one out of high school by the Tampa Bay Devil Rays and considered a can't-miss prospect. Within three years he was addicted to crack cocaine and was out of baseball after failing repeated drug tests. Josh is a big man, standing about six feet four, and very strong. But at his lowest point, his tattoo-covered body had dwindled from 230 pounds to 180. His life was in a horrible downward spiral that he had to pull out of or he would die. Josh once described himself as "a dead man walking" after he found himself walking along the double yellow line in the middle of a busy highway with traffic speeding past on either side.

And then his life miraculously changed. After his grandmother confronted him in October 2005, Josh gave his life to Christ, and he received the supernatural help to turn his life around. His wife, Katie, who had done her best to stand by him during the years of his addiction, forgave him and sought to restore their marriage.

In 2007 the Cincinnati Reds signed Josh to a Major League contract, and his first Major League hit was a home run. A year later, after being traded to the Texas Rangers, he set a record in the home run derby before the 2008 All-Star Game by hitting twenty-eight homers in the first round. This was a man who had hit rock bottom just a few years before. He had come all the way back.

But what makes this story even more amazing is that Katie, who had every reason not to forgive him after all he had put her through, did forgive him and worked to restore their marriage to where it is today: a shining example of love, reconciliation, and forgiveness.

God loves to restore us! He loves to turn our sinful rebellion into miracles. And if God can turn these failures into miracles, surely He can do something wonderful with your mistakes.

WHEN COMMITMENTS ARE BROKEN

✦ JAMES

When commitments are broken, we believe the best thing you can do is offer forgiveness and grace, both to yourself and to your spouse. We're not suggesting you put on a brave face and hope everything will get better. No, we're talking about real, substantial, deep healing and restoration. We're talking about dealing with the root of the problems between you and your spouse and bringing the healing power of God to bear on your situation.

In order for that to work, you have to want to get well. You have to be willing to do whatever it takes to heal your relationship, and sometimes that means drastic action. If the struggle is with pornography, substance addiction, or unbridled anger, most likely it will be necessary to get outside assistance, counseling, and intervention.

When dealing with such issues, it is important to be able to share with your spouse how difficult and painful it is to live in defeat. Everyone understands the pain of the mate who's been betrayed or let down, but the pain that led to the problem in the first place must also be addressed. The defeated person will often be seeking a shoulder to cry on, someone who will not throw stones and join in the offense.

If you're the spouse who has been betrayed, it is very important that you draw on your commitment to love your spouse through this difficult season and not heap shame upon him or her. It's amazing how some people look for faults in others as if they'll be rewarded for finding them. But when you're down, you'll find it difficult to do right when all you hear is what's wrong. A poor self-image is fed by a lack of unconditional love. Husbands and wives should provide the safest possible place for their spouse to seek refuge. The promise of freedom is too important to be set aside or taken lightly.

When commitments have been broken, both parties need healing. The one being forgiven must realize and understand the hurt experienced by the one who was betrayed. It takes time for both spouses to heal. One is waiting to be healed and forgiven; the other is forgiving the hurt but also needing healing of her or his heart. The forgiven one often wants to forget what has happened, but the one who has been hurt still wants and needs to heal, because forgetting is difficult.

If you have a recurring pattern of defeat or betrayal in your marriage, it will be difficult to address these issues without outside help. We encourage you to seek a counselor or therapist who can help you get to the root of your problem and begin to rebuild your marriage on a solid foundation. A counselor might also help you establish healthy boundaries for your marriage, which may facilitate the process of restoring trust and communication.

The first step in any marriage revival, of course, is deciding that your marriage is worth fighting for, that it's worth going the extra mile. If your spouse has failed, you can take on the responsibilities of a covenant relationship by offering forgiveness and strength to help lift your mate out of defeat and lift your relationship out of failure and despair. Restoration is always available and always possible as long as both of you desire it and are willing to submit yourselves to God to bring it about.

> *Restoration is always available and always possible.*

A WORD TO THE DIVORCED AND TO THOSE CONSIDERING DIVORCE

Perhaps you've already experienced a divorce, or maybe your marriage is teetering on the brink. What kinds of reconciliation and restoration are possible for you? Is there ever a time divorce is okay? Does getting a divorce mean you're giving up and not letting God make a miracle out of your mistake?

Betty and I are hurt by the thought of any divorce. Although we never want to see it happen, we understand that it does happen, and this is always a tragedy. We don't believe divorce is the will of God, but we see that Scripture makes a provision—because of the hardness of the human heart—for a divorce to be granted.

I'm not going to discuss the many theological views on divorce here, but I can tell you what I've come to understand as I've studied the Scriptures and prayed about this crucial issue. When the Bible says in Malachi 2:16 that God hates divorce, I believe what He really hates are the circumstances in a relationship that lead to a divorce. A divorce decree is just a piece of paper that a couple gets from a courthouse, but the actual divorce happens long before the certificate is issued. God hates anything that damages the joyful, meaningful relationship He intends for a husband and wife to experience in marriage. God designed the one-flesh, one-spirit, leaving-and-cleaving marriage relationship so that couples, in their togetherness, would reflect His character and nature more fully. So anything that undermines a marriage is contrary to God's purpose and design. That's why He feels so strongly about preserving and defending marriages.

Even if you're not divorced on paper but you're divorced in your attitude toward your spouse or you're living in separate worlds while coexisting under the same roof, you're every bit as much in need of God's healing power as a couple that has received a divorce decree. As noble as it may seem, if you're gritting your teeth and saying to yourself, "I may be unhappy, but I'm not getting a divorce," you're missing out on God's best design for your marriage. God doesn't want you to settle for second best. He wants to demonstrate His power through your weakness and make your marriage into a shining example of His redemptive and healing power.

Are you willing to pursue that? Your marriage can become all you've ever hoped for as well as all that God intends it to be.

Granted, it's very difficult, if not impossible, to preserve your commitment if your spouse is rebellious, indifferent, insensitive, or unwilling to change. No one said it was going to be easy. But because Betty and I have seen the power of prayer transform even the hardest of hearts, our encouragement to you is this: don't give up! We've seen that when some couples hit their lowest point, the offending party realizes his or her mistake and makes a turnaround. Of course, we've also seen some relationships end in divorce at this point, which breaks our hearts.

Those who have no interest in turning from their destructive ways must, through the prayers of others, be turned over to God. Ultimately, they are responsible for their own actions; it is not our responsibility to change our loved ones. We can try to have a positive influence, but in the end it's up to them to seek God for the necessary changes. Pressure, nagging, complaints, criticism, scolding, and similar actions aren't going to do a thing. Instead, pray that you'll see something supernatural happen. Your mate has the capacity to change, but he or she can't be beaten into restoration. Instead, he or she must be invited into it and must openly welcome the necessary changes.

But what if you've already gone through a divorce? Does this mean that God no longer loves you or that you've failed in such a horrible way there's no hope for the future or for a meaningful life? Absolutely not! In many ways a divorce is like a traffic accident. Betty and I believe that we are to treat people who've been through the wreck of divorce the same way we would treat someone who has been in a physical accident. We must assess the damage and then work to restore the injured parties and build them up individually and collectively.

God doesn't want you to settle for second best.

We have found that those who see their marriages restored and those who discover a meaningful relationship and future after divorce have some things in common. They truly learn from their past mistakes and poor judgment. Regardless of who was at fault, they commit their lives totally to God's will and His direction for their future. They discover that God does, in fact, make all things new when they totally submit themselves to the skillful hands of the Master Potter. All observers will soon see a vessel shaped to honor God.

FOR REFLECTION AND DISCUSSION

Why is a broken commitment such a serious matter?

If a close friend suffered a broken commitment, how would you advise him or her to respond?

PART 3

Communication

8

Communication

Openly say what you mean and

mean what you say—in love.

JAMES

Communication—both verbal and nonverbal—ties together the inner qualities of two people in a marriage. Communication is what makes commitment, trust, and concern visible in a marriage, and in that way it's a reflection of those inner qualities. If you're committed to your spouse, concerned about your spouse, and both trusting and trustworthy with your spouse, you're well on your way to having good communication, because all the necessary pieces are in place.

When we say *communication*, we don't mean talking to make your opinion heard. Creating an open channel for direct, straightforward communication involves both talking and listening, giving and receiving. This type of communication is essential to living in love.

An important thing to remember is that communication is not something you do only when you need to have a talk. Rather, communication is constantly happening. Whether it's having a simple conversation or laughing together, smiling at each other across the dinner table or putting your arm around your spouse's shoulders, hiding behind the newspaper or banging pots and pans in the kitchen—all these things are communication.

According to Albert Mehrabian and Susan R. Ferris, "Studies have shown that 55 percent of impact is determined by body language; 38 percent by tone of voice; and 7 percent by the content or words used in the communication process."[1] Words are important to communication, but so are vocal inflections, tone, gestures, facial expressions, posture, eye contact, and a host of other nonverbal cues. All these cues contribute to the overall quality and effectiveness of communication. You can tell your spouse "I love you" all day long, but if you say it with slumped shoulders, a hung head, and no zeal, it's going to have a different meaning than a heartfelt "I love you."

So if you are constantly communicating with your spouse, the question then becomes, What are you communicating? Does the expression on your face give you away? The prophet Isaiah answers, "The expression of their faces bears witness against them" (3:9, NASB). If you're happy in your marriage, do your face and body language show it?

We aren't suggesting that you put on a brave face to cover up discontent. If you're unhappy, you need to address it and deal with it. We're simply pointing out that when it comes to communication with your mate, words are not enough.

BE OPEN AND HONEST

We cannot overstate the importance of clear, honest, and open dialogue. This means discussing things as they come up and without holding on to your anger or frustrations. It means working as much or more to hear your spouse as you work to make yourself heard. You don't withhold information from each other, but instead lay everything on the table: the good, the bad, and the ugly.

Open, honest communication enables you to love each other through your differences. Instead of approaching communication with the attitude that "I'm going to set you straight and show you I know more about this than you do," the two of you should agree to seek both under-standing and humility. Betty and I approach com-munication with the attitude that "your feelings are valid, and you must have them for a reason, so let's get to the bottom of this disagreement or mis-understanding."

Facial expressions and body language often speak louder than words.

Done properly, communication will always include love, understanding, and a willingness to listen to each other's heart. And remember, facial expressions and body language often speak louder than words.

FOCUS ON TEAMWORK

✦ BETTY

James always uses his hands for emphasis, and it's very easy to read his facial ex-pressions. One of our staff members once told him that he had shouted at her. He responded, "I don't recall ever raising my voice at you." She answered, "Yes, but you've given me loud looks!"

I think the key to effective communication is to remember that you and your spouse are on the same team. Teamwork is important even in the way you speak to each other. Joking around is one thing, but when you have legitimate disagreements, you need to remember that ultimately you're both on the same side.

James and I still strongly disagree from time to time, as any couple does, but in the midst of those heated discussions, I'm not going to say something de-liberately hurtful to him just so I can make a point or win an argument. What would that accomplish? But I'm not perfect, and I might still make a cutting remark. If I have that level of frustration or anger within me, our disagreement is certainly a "we" problem in that it affects James as much as it affects me. So it's something we need to work through together. Then we can focus on being a team and on getting through to each other.

If you find you're prone to attack your spouse with words, remember this advice from Proverbs 12:18: "Some people make cutting remarks, but the words of the wise bring healing."

If your spouse is really stuck on an issue and doesn't want to talk about it but you really want to help, the best thing you can do is pray about your side of the equation and trust God to deal with your spouse. You might not be able to discuss it with your spouse at that moment, but don't let that stop you from seeking God and saying, *Lord, change everything in me that needs to be changed. And let me be so filled with Your light and Your love that maybe it will influence my mate, who's really struggling right now.*

When push comes to shove, focus on surrendering your own will and desires to God, because you can't change the other person. God has to do that. If you're berating or nagging your spouse and putting him or her down, it's only going to make things worse. If, instead, you'll start with your own heart and say, *God, change me and make me all You want me to be,* and if you'll then trust God to deal with your spouse, He will honor that choice and respond.

✦ JAMES

Betty is certainly right about this. The apostle Peter says that the greatest dress a woman can wear is the "unfading beauty of a gentle and quiet spirit."[2] He says it will win over her husband, even if he is resistant to hearing biblical truth.[3]

There is something very powerful about a woman who has a gentle and quiet spirit. That doesn't mean she submits herself to being run over. It doesn't make her a doormat. It doesn't mean not standing up for what's right and making her views known. It does mean that she submits herself to God first and foremost and trusts Him to deal with her husband.

During our most heated discussions, Betty's quiet spirit and sweet heart cause me to want to seek reconciliation when we disagree. She inspires me to search my own heart to find solutions. It's not as if we're suiting up to go into a boxing ring, but we can have some pretty forceful conversations. Yet Betty's gentle spirit, even when she's standing her ground and making her point, causes me not only to increase in sensitivity but to desire to become even more sensitive, both to God and to Betty.

As a matter of fact, because I know that Betty's basic nature is to be timid and shy, I'll encourage her—even in the midst of a good argument—to stick to her guns and express herself. If she's not just responding in anger or the heat of the moment, I might even say, "That's good! Now you're making your point, and I'm hearing you." She and I find it very inviting to grow like that in our relationship, to the point that we can enjoy and preserve our commitment to each other even when we're temporarily at odds.

Unfortunately, many couples enter into marriage with the opposite mentality and foolishly decide to work against each other. If you think of your relationship as a competition between you and your mate that only one of you can win, the strength of your marriage will be undermined.

This is especially true when it comes to communication. It is extremely easy to fall into a pattern of trying to win arguments with your spouse. But if you have this mind-set in your marriage, you'll end up losing even when you believe you've won. By crushing your spouse's feelings in order to make your own feelings superior, you have weakened your commitment. You have taken your marriage off the solid foundation of dedication and placed it on the shifting sands of a competitive, self-serving spirit. How can you be happy if you're actively working against your own joy and competing with the very person you love most? There simply isn't a way to live for yourself within a marriage and maintain happiness and harmony with your spouse.

Betty and I have learned over the years that, if we're going to thrive, we must approach our commitment to each other as an act of teamwork. We are in this relationship together, and we will either succeed together, or we will fail together. We will not be divided by anyone, including our children, who have always known that their mom and dad are a team—truly one—and will not be pitted against each other.

TALK THINGS OUT

✦ BETTY

Part of the strength of our commitment is that we have never thought about not being married to each other. That doesn't mean we don't have differences, disagreements, and heated discussions. It doesn't mean we don't have times when we don't like being around each other for the moment. I think the difference is that we know we are going to stay together, and we both want to have a good marriage.

Because of James's determination to talk about our problems until they are resolved (a character quality that had to come from God, because nothing in James's upbringing would have taught him to hang in there and work things out), I learned how to open up and express my feelings. If it had been left up to me, I would not have done it. It wasn't in my nature to talk things out. I was a pouter, and I could pout really, really well. But because James is a confronter, he does not let things lie. He will say, "Even if it takes us days or weeks, we're going to keep talking about this until we work it out and reach a conclusion—until we agree about how to handle it."

I had never been around a two-sided confrontation before. I would hear Mom and Dad argue—mainly Mom—but I never heard them really work things out. To be fair, I feel Mom wanted to engage in open communication, but Dad didn't know how. Out of frustration she would get angry and shout to be heard. That approach was not the best. James, however, was determined that, with both of us talking about whatever the situation was, we would get through it.

We haven't always done it smoothly, and at times it is a real struggle. We might go through a time when we have to step back to get some perspective or to give the other person room to breathe, but then we come at the issue again and try to reach an agreement. It has often been painful for me, but I'm grateful that James doesn't allow things to build up inside either of us, where they might grow out of proportion.

✦ JAMES

We don't want to give the impression that we had a perfect relationship from the get-go, because we didn't. I do think, however, that we have worked at our problems correctly by tackling them as a couple and really trying to hear each other, which is the communication style of appropriate confrontation. But in the early days of our relationship when I could tell that Betty wasn't going to listen, it really burned me. She wouldn't listen and wouldn't talk. She just wanted to go into a corner and pout. Or she would storm into the bedroom and slam the door. Often I would hop in the car and drive off, which truly was an immature response. But it was my way of responding to Betty's withdrawal from the conversation. I thought, *If that's how you want to be, I'll put even more distance between us.*

I think I drove off more for the shock effect, because I always turned around in a relatively short time and came back. If you go off and seethe, that's when the other person begins to feel deeply hurt. So the fact that I turned around and came back right away was an indication that God had given me enough sensitivity and insight to think, *Hey, don't behave that way. Resolving your differences is more important than feeding your petty, foolish feelings.*

By the time I returned, Betty was usually out of the bedroom, or wherever she had gone, and she was glad to see me. And I was happy to see her with a little different attitude. But we finally realized that putting distance between ourselves by going down the road, extending the time when we acted as if we couldn't care less, or feeling angry was not a healthy way to solve our problems.

We still have times when Betty will walk away from me or I'll get upset and walk to the other end of the room or around the corner and maybe shout something silly back at her. But we don't stay in that mood for long, because we're just not going to live in conflict with each other.

Our commitment is to deal with our disagreements and not to wrangle over words. As Paul reminded Timothy, "Avoid worthless, foolish talk that only leads to more godless behavior. This kind of talk spreads like cancer."[4] "Foolish talk" can mean a whole lot more than arguing about Scripture. It also includes endless wrangling over positions, words, and opinions. We're seeing it right now in our country. It wearies me to see the level of public discourse, the way opposing sides talk about each other with such disdain. It's foolish, worthless, and malignant.

> *Our commitment is to deal with our disagreements and not to wrangle over words.*

In a marriage it's important to recognize that your words can create distance between you and your spouse, but you cannot leave that distance there. Issues and hurts must be addressed, and proper confrontation is imperative. Let me gratefully add that through God's grace, I have become a more compassionate confronter.

WATCH HOW YOU SPEAK

✦ BETTY

I think we came to realize that our tone of voice when we had disagreements really set the stage for whether we were going to listen to each other or not. If we came at it in anger or in frustration or with accusations, instead of with a listening heart, we knew we would never get far in the discussion. We had to remind ourselves that we were not each other's enemy. We might be trying to get a point across or a different opinion on a particular point, but our opinions were not going to be heard if we came at each other with sharp words and the wrong tone of voice.

It's possible to confront someone without really communicating. You can spill out all your emotions and anger and frustration and not get anywhere. If you can engage each other in a civil manner, you're much more likely to hear and be heard. When the temperature in an argument begins to rise, take a moment to back off and cool down. When you're ready to listen with an open mind and heart, say, "Okay, tell me. I'm ready to listen with my heart."

When James and I disagree, we're less concerned about holding to our respective positions and more concerned about understanding why we disagree. When I feel as if James is really listening to my heart and not just trying to win the argument or put me in my place, I'm free to open up and trust him with my ideas and opinions. Because I know he cares, I can be confident that I won't be humiliated. He's not going to hear me out and then respond in frustration and anger and tell me, "You're flat-out wrong!" Instead, we'll both be able to trust our heart with each other, pray together, and come to a sensible conclusion.

I do believe God has given James compassion when he confronts, and He has given me an understanding of its importance. The next chapter is dedicated to this very important practice of confrontation.

DON'T LET THE SUN SET ON YOUR ANGER

✦ JAMES

The best advice we received before our wedding was from Betty's older sister, Marjorie, who had married a few years earlier. She encouraged us to take Ephesians 4:26–27 to heart and make it a centerpiece of our marriage: "Don't let the sun go down while you are still angry, for anger gives a foothold to the devil."

Little did we realize just how important these verses would be to our marriage. Betty and I made a commitment to each other to communicate no matter what and never go to sleep angry. But as I have often joked, "There were times when we wouldn't sleep for three weeks!"

Actually, we'd sometimes lie on either side of the bed and pretend we were asleep. I would even throw in a fake snore or two to seal the deal. Eventually, however, one of us would nudge the other, and we'd roll over and start talking. We both acknowledge how happy we are when the other person reaches out with a loving touch.

In forty-seven years of marriage, I can honestly say we've never gone to sleep without coming to a peaceful solution, even if that solution was that we needed to think about our disagreement for a while and take it up later in order to determine the best course of action. Not once have we gone to sleep angry with each other. I believe the power of that commitment is greater than we can possibly convey in a book.

If you and your spouse have been turning your backs on each other and going to sleep angry or hurt, you need to look each other in the eye and say, "You know what? That's a really bad practice. Let's agree never to do it again." When you let anger, frustration, and pain lodge in your heart, when you stew in your own juices instead of dealing with your problems openly and honestly, your anger can become a root of bitterness. After the seeds of disappointment, pain, anger, and grief take root and sprout, eventually they will produce a crop of even greater disappointment, pain, anger, and grief. And gradually, over time, your heart will harden.

I've heard medical doctors say that when you hold on to anger or become bitter, something happens in your entire body that's harmful to the healing process—it jams your system both physically and mentally. A psychologist appearing on *Life Today* said that unresolved anger and other negative habits and addictions create a type of abscess in the human brain. People with deeply rooted bitterness and addictive practices can have what appears to be a bruise on their brain, which is visible on some scans.[5]

It is important for you to take care of negative feelings and emotions as they arise, and this can be done only through open and honest communication, including necessary confrontation. That doesn't mean, however, that every discussion has to take place immediately.

I heard of a couple who has worked out an agreement that allows the wife—

who is quiet and reflective—to formulate her thoughts before she engages in complex discussions with her husband, who is more verbal and quick on his feet. When the wife feels pressured, she'll say, "Can we talk about this in an hour?" or whatever time seems appropriate. This technique gives her time to prepare, but it also assures her husband that the conversation will take place eventually and won't be swept under the rug.

Early on, when Betty would get hurt and go to the other end of the house to pout, I knew that style of communication wasn't going to work. I knew we would never sort things out if she wanted to close herself off while I wanted to express myself and be heard. Instead, we had to agree to open communication. It was the only way to work through the stresses and strains of those early days. Although we would often reach a push-and-shove point where we both were trying to make a case for our own perspectives, we still had a commitment to listen and be heard in order to get to the root of the problem.

It is imperative to the success of your marriage to keep the lines of communication open. Refusing to discuss an issue or resorting to the silent treatment is like allowing carbon monoxide to fill a room. Eventually the poison of hurt, pain, and a closed-off attitude will suffocate your relationship. When you stop sharing openly, you stop living and begin merely existing. To refuse to communicate is to accept a form of bondage that, if allowed to take hold, will become in many ways a prison. Sadly, when I observe married couples, it seems many of them are rapidly approaching this situation.

After nearly fifty years of being married, we are still perfecting our ability to communicate openly. It was a great idea way back when, and it's still a great idea today!

Learn the Communication Three-Step

Over the years Betty and I have discovered three simple steps that help us immeasurably in keeping our communication flowing and growing: stop, repeat, clarify.

When we're trying to make a point or just make ourselves heard, it's easy and tempting to get on a roll, talking and talking and talking without taking time to really listen. So Betty and I, before we get to that point, always try to stop ourselves in order to hear the other person's heart, not just the words. We stop and take time to listen.

Then, if we're unsure if we've been heard, we repeat ourselves, usually expounding on whatever feeling or thought we were initially discussing. By repeating and expanding, we're able to better express our heart to each other. We repeat until we are hearing far more than mere words. Heart harmony is our goal.

After this step we put into our own words what the other person is saying—to make sure we heard each other's heart correctly. It's easy to misunderstand a certain word or phrase or to twist it in a direction that the one speaking didn't intend, so this clarification is essential for putting us both on the same page. We clarify until we're certain we've both heard and understood each other's thoughts and intentions.

Stop. Repeat. Clarify. With these three vital steps, we've ended the times when we would snap at each other for no real reason, when a simple statement like "Why did you say that?" could turn into an even more heated discussion.

DIAGNOSING YOUR DIFFICULTIES

✦ BETTY

It is incredibly easy to allow small issues to hinder communication but sometimes difficult to notice those obstacles. James and I have struggled through these problems before, and I've thought a lot about ways to diagnose what prevents us from communicating effectively.

The first obstacle is worrying about who's right and who's wrong. In most cases that leads only to frustration and pain. Typically, in our relationship, anytime we encounter an issue that leads to an argument, I can look back later and see how we were both right in some respects and both wrong in others. Playing the blame game is not only fruitless but endless. Remember, you're on the same team, so act like it. Put aside issues of right and wrong and strive instead for the common goal of living in love. Because we are truly one in Christ and in marriage, we must strive to "preserve the unity of the Spirit in the bond of peace."[6]

Obviously, there are extreme instances, such as abuse or infidelity, in which one spouse can be completely out of God's will. In those cases it is often necessary to seek outside help in order to be restored in your relationship with God and with your spouse. I would never counsel someone to stay with a dangerously abusive spouse who shows no remorse for his or her actions. But in most cases and in most relationships, I have observed that small incidents spiral out of control because the couple is arguing more about who is right than what is right.

Beware of another major obstacle to communication: the inability to listen to the other person. I've witnessed many times when couples were talking and neither one was really listening. Instead, both were just waiting out the other person's monologue so they could say their own piece and get across their own point. This tactic is the complete opposite of communicating.

Instead, we need to cultivate a desire to listen to and truly hear the other person. As James stated earlier, we need to learn to stop, repeat, and clarify. Listening to your spouse isn't going to come naturally all the time; you have to intentionally work at it with determination.

And as long as you're working on listening, you can work on another obstacle to communication: an unwillingness to forgive your spouse when he or she has wronged you or failed you in some way. We see this obstacle often in our culture, but it is especially damaging in a marriage relationship. Jesus said plainly that we are all sinners who need to be forgiven, and if we cannot forgive others, then God will not forgive us (see Matthew 6:14–15). Withholding forgiveness doesn't hurt your spouse—it hurts you.

Unforgiveness also gets in the way of your communication, because it becomes a filter through which you hear every word your spouse says to you. And then you won't be able to hear his or her heart in the slightest. All you will hear are your own hurt and anger. By offering forgiveness, you clear the channels of communication and eliminate the unreliable filter.

Another obstacle I had in my relationship with James dovetails with this: sometimes I wouldn't forgive myself. I wouldn't want to admit wrongdoing in any situation, because I felt as if admitting I was wrong was the same as admitting failure. Of course, nothing could be further from the truth. Admitting to wrongdoing is simply admitting to being human. Your spouse is human as well. You both mess up. By admitting this and seeking out what is right rather than who is right, you will remove this obstacle to clear communication.

GETTING BEYOND A CONFLICT

Now let's consider some ways in which we can resolve our conflicts and get the answers we need.

For starters, one thing James and I discovered early on is to remember how much we love each other. James never misses an opportunity to tell me how much he loves me. Not a day goes by without his taking time to think of me, notice me, and say something about it to me. Throughout the day he continually tells me that I'm pretty and that he loves me.

Even when he traveled all the time, James would call me at least twice a day just to chat and keep up with me. I may have been home alone, but knowing I was in his thoughts did wonders for me and kept our communication alive. These types of appreciative gestures—phone calls, love notes, occasional surprises—are very important in maintaining an open channel of clear communication.

We have learned to listen with an open heart, and we try to never put down anything the other person says. Instead of interrupting each other in the midst of a heated discussion, we let the other person share from the heart. By treating everything as important and worth listening to, we constantly affirm each other's ideas, desires, and point of view, which is essential to good communication.

Another key to successful communication is constantly encouraging, appreciating, and recognizing each other's abilities. I always affirm James's gifts, and he does the same for me. This has helped me, especially since I had such low self-esteem when we were first married. I couldn't discover the gifts God had given me. But through James's encouragement and his belief and trust in me, I began to see the things God had put in my heart, along with all the ways He wanted to use my gifts to bless others.

The final step to removing communication obstacles requires a mental shovel: you have to learn to bury mistakes. When your spouse has hurt you, it's important to forgive. But you can't stop there; you must also take the next step and bury the hurtful behavior. If he or she has apologized for it, you need to forget it, bury it, and move on. Don't bring up those past mistakes in the midst of a later argument.

The Bible tells us in Isaiah 43:25 that God "will blot out [our] sins for [His] own sake and will never think of them again." You've heard the phrase "forgive and forget." We encourage you to do the same thing when it comes to your spouse, especially because this is how God treats you.

✦ JAMES

Even after nearly fifty years with this type of commitment and communication, Betty and I still find things we could argue about every day. We still don't say everything exactly the way we should, and we're continually working to be heard and understood. It's easy to be abrupt, impatient, or harsh with each other even when we know we're out of line. We have to continually remind ourselves to stop, repeat, and clarify. Even though we still don't communicate perfectly, it is possible and important to learn how to argue in a healthy manner.

There is no shortcut to success. Creating a flow of honest communication with each other is going to take time and commitment. But if there's any relationship worth working on, worth living out, it's your marriage. Apart from your relationship with God, your relationship with your spouse should be life's most joyful experience.

FOR REFLECTION AND DISCUSSION

What are some ways you communicate without actually using words?

Why is it hard to listen in the middle of a verbal conflict?

What does it mean to listen with your heart?

9

Confrontation

Speak the truth in love.

BETTY

ommunicating well with your spouse will at times mean gently pointing out something that bothers you. If your relationship is firmly rooted in a lifelong commitment to each other and you've worked to build up concern for each other and trust in your marriage, it's possible to confront important issues without blowing the wheels off the wagon. That doesn't mean it won't sometimes be painful or difficult for both of you, but it does mean you have the freedom to speak the truth in love.[1]

When I was growing up, my shy personality helped me to unintentionally create an image of myself as a sweet girl who never did anything wrong. This self-image caused me to try to hide my flaws and hope that everybody would love the sweet person they saw, because they certainly wouldn't like the fearful person I really was. I built a wall of defense around myself, because I believed that if the real me were ever exposed, everyone would think I was ugly and stupid. But hiding myself didn't work very well. For example, when I was in junior high, one of the girls at school told my best friend she thought I was stuck-up. I cried when I heard that, because all she saw was the wall I had built to protect myself.

The truth is, I wasn't prideful; I was fearful. I walked in perpetual fear that people wouldn't love me if they found out that I didn't match up with their image of me. Imagine taking that kind of fear into a marriage relationship, where hiding it would be impossible. I knew that sooner or later James would see the real me. What would he think of me then?

This fear made it extremely difficult for me to open up to James and admit my problems. I didn't want to share my struggles with him because I was so afraid of being exposed as unworthy. As a result I didn't want anyone—least of all my husband—to know about my fear. I figured this was just the way life was going to be for me and that if I didn't talk about my fear, it would eventually go away. All I had to do was hang in there until Jesus came back.

✦ JAMES

Part of the reason Betty was not focusing much on her own fear and other issues was that she was taking such good care of me! During this time I was struggling mightily myself, and because of her deep concern for my needs, she neglected her own spiritual growth while keeping up appearances as a loyal, churchgoing wife and mother.

When I had my spiritual breakthrough and Betty saw me find new joy and peace in my relationship with God, her feelings of inadequacy were provoked, and she shut down. That's when she began experiencing severe, debilitating headaches and often feeling tired, weak, and worthless. Neither one of us understood there was a powerful enemy in the spiritual realm of darkness continually attacking us. (We will share important insights concerning this spiritual warfare in chapter 15.)

✦ BETTY

Fortunately, James was patient with me. Even though he could see the fear all over me, he waited on the Lord to work in my life. It got to the point where I actually became afraid of God's Word. Although I was reading my Bible every day, it was just words on a page, words for someone else, not for me. I was trying to find peace in my own strength, but I had a mental block: I wasn't allowing God to speak to me through His Word.

Eventually my fear became so overwhelming that I started having frequent, extremely painful headaches. Many afternoons the children would come home from school and find me lying on the sofa. When they would ask, "Mom, why do you always have a headache?" I didn't have an answer.

One evening as I was lying on the sofa with a headache, I became desperate enough to try to talk to James about what was going on. I looked over and asked him, "Do you hear God saying anything about me?"

James calmly left his chair, came over, and sat down beside me. He put his arm around me and said, "Honey, you're not going to like this, but God has shown me you have an unteachable spirit."

All of a sudden I was full of energy. I sat straight up, not believing what he had just said. For a person dealing with a terrible headache, I didn't act like it at that moment. I jumped up angrily and stormed out of the room. James was right, but I sure didn't like hearing it!

James knew I needed some time alone, and he wisely left the house, taking the kids to the park while I stayed in our bedroom by myself. He knew what I needed to do, and somehow I did too. With the house quiet, I got down on my knees and desperately cried out to God: "Is what James said true?"

Immediately God spoke to my heart: Yes, you do have an unteachable spirit.

Those words from the Lord hurt, and I began to pray with a broken heart, finally admitting my fear to God and deciding to be released from that stronghold right then. I determined to be totally submitted to God's will and to allow Him to make any necessary changes in my life. I needed to be confronted, and James did it in love. Ultimately, love won.

Because of my fear and the walls I had built to try to protect myself from judgment and rejection, it was very important how James approached me when I asked him that question. He could have shaken his finger in my face or raised his voice and done his best to put me in my place, but he didn't. I already felt that if anyone saw me as I really was, they wouldn't like me or they would think I was dumb. So if James had attacked or ridiculed me, he would have made my situation and the battle raging inside me even worse. His loving, soft response was the perfect balm for someone who had already beaten herself up for many years. The tenderness and compassion that James displayed opened the door for God to speak to my heart and change me.

CONFRONTATION IS NECESSARY AND GOOD

✦ JAMES

Confrontation can often be uncomfortable, even if your relationship is generally in a good place or if you're having a good day. Sometimes the last thing you want to do is wreck a good feeling by bringing up a frustration or an area of concern in your marriage. But confrontation is necessary. Think of it as a type of pressure valve. The same way that a valve relieves high pressure in a closed system to prevent damage, confrontation is a great way to release tension in your relationship. By dealing with frustrations and anger through focused confrontation before they build up, you activate your relationship's pressure valve and prevent the possibility of serious damage to your marriage. Remember, it is hidden damage that often leads to a blowout.

In the Bible, God often uses confrontation to bring to light things that need to be dealt with. One clear example is the situation after David had sinned with Bathsheba and then had her husband, Uriah, killed to cover up her pregnancy.

This terrible travesty was exposed through confrontation. David thought he had gotten away with his sin until God sent the prophet Nathan to confront him (see 2 Samuel 12). Nathan appeared before David and told a story of two men. One was rich; the other was poor. The rich man had plenty, but the poor man had only one little lamb that meant everything to him.

In Nathan's confrontational story, the rich man needed to make a meal for a traveler, but instead of using his own resources, he stole the poor man's only lamb. David became enraged upon hearing the story and called down condemnation on the rich man.

Then Nathan struck the telling blow, revealing that David himself was the rich man who had despised all God had given him and had taken what didn't belong to him: Uriah's wife. This act of confrontation stirred David's conscience and brought conviction and immediate repentance. Because of David's repentance, God blessed him with another son, Solomon, who went on to have a great legacy by passing on words of wisdom capable of inspiring success in all areas of life. Through the psalms of David, you can find comfort and insight for all of life's challenges. He can help lead you from the pit of despair to the pinnacle of praise.

Confrontation is a great way to release tension in your relationship.

What can we learn from this biblical story of confrontation? We see the prophet Nathan doing what is right in God's eyes while putting his life on the line by telling King David something he would not want to hear. Perhaps Nathan used the form of a story, like a parable, in order to confront David in a more palatable way.

Even so, the prophet was direct and to the point, but he also understood the need to confront David in a way that David would receive the confrontation. If he'd strolled into the throne room and told David directly what had happened, he would have surely been killed. Instead, he spoke in a language that David, a former shepherd boy, would understand: sheep. David understood the mind-set of the poor shepherd. By confronting David with just such a story, Nathan was able to relate the sin to David in a way that would get through to him and bring about repentance and resolution.

Likewise, we speak of confrontation as a means of listening to your spouse's heart and expressing your own heart in a way that will ring loud and clear. It isn't always comfortable, but it is always necessary.

CONFRONTATION IS INEVITABLE

Many couples see confrontation as fighting, but to Betty and me, *confrontation* is a positive word. The key, I think, is that we don't confront each other; we confront the problem or the attitude that would otherwise hinder or stop the flow of open, honest communication. Instead of letting ourselves stew silently in our frustration, hurt, or doubt, we confront those feelings by thoroughly addressing them with each other. We rely on the trust and goodwill we've built up in our relationship over the years to be the oil that keeps the gears of communication meshing smoothly, even when the heat is on.

This is especially true when it comes to confrontation, which inevitably will occur in your marriage. The fact is this: confrontation must be adopted as a necessary practice. The word *confrontation* often brings up mental images of war and strife, heated quarrels and painful conflict, but we want you to see it in a different way. Betty and I think of confrontation as a way of taking the bull by the horns to ensure we are being heard in the way we want to be heard and as a step toward abiding peace.

> *We go to war against our human tendency to avoid responsibility and our natural unwillingness to admit wrongdoing.*

Too often, confrontation is seen as an attempt to set the other person straight. Instead, we're suggesting that it's a way of honest communication. There's a big difference between being assertive and being aggressive. *Assertiveness* means speaking the truth in love: saying what you need to say directly and in a loving manner. *Aggressiveness* tries to take a piece out of the other person while communicating thoughts and feelings in an inappropriate manner. When confrontation is done right, it will preserve both the relationship *and* the message you want to convey.

Betty and I try, in particular, to confront any attitudes of selfishness and blame shifting. We go to war against our human tendency to avoid responsibility and our natural unwillingness to admit wrongdoing. We fight against frustration and anger, not against each other. And we do this by taking a stand while sharing our hearts with each other. We talk openly and listen attentively. We deal with what we know to be necessary in healthy confrontation.

If your spouse has hurt you or disappointed you enough that it sticks in your mind (or in your craw), then the situation must be confronted. But keep in mind, how you confront is every bit as important as what you confront.

CONFRONT WITH CARE

✦ BETTY

Being confronted or confronting a problem or person was never easy for me. But I thank God I came to understand its importance. A vital step in confronting each other is developing a willingness to listen. And when I say "listen," I don't mean just hearing the other person's words. I mean really listening to hear the depth of the other person's heart. For open and honest communication to work, we must treat our spouse's thoughts, words, and feelings with the same respect we want for our own.

It's very important that we never put down what our spouse says, because this will only close off the desire to share whatever hurts or concerns she or he might be feeling. Instead, when you and your spouse are talking things out, do your best to put aside whatever anger or frustration you may be feeling and really listen, the same way you want her or him to listen to your heart.

Another important step in confrontation is prayer. Ask God to give you ears to hear the intentions of your spouse's heart. Ask God to give you the right words to convey what's on your heart. And ask Him to bless your marriage and help you protect the relationship you so deeply desire and cherish.

In my initial confrontations with James, I really felt lost. James is a gifted communicator, but he didn't handle everything well when it came to conflict resolution. Thankfully, he was wise enough to know the importance of dealing with the real issue. So, for example, I was able to look past his mistakes and see his basic conviction about not letting the sun go down on our anger. Even if I might be really angry about something, I knew it was important to our relationship for us to stay in communication until we worked things out satisfactorily. On the other hand, I believed I was not a very good communicator because I wasn't quick with words. Learning how to share my heart and my inner fears with my husband not only felt difficult but intimidating. I had to practice and work hard at it. Although direct confrontation came naturally to James, it was a style of communication I had not experienced.

I had a tendency to withdraw, to let things fester while I pouted. When we got into a heated discussion or James did or said something I didn't agree with, my natural reaction was to get tight-lipped and solitary. I would quietly stew, hoping things would just go away. Instead, the opposite happened. My frustrations did not dissipate; they built up inside me, ready to explode.

Fortunately, James encouraged confrontation. He knew that his gift of authoritative communication could have steamrolled my naturally shy and tender heart. He could have seen my timidity and pounced on it, trying to become the lord over our home. He could have easily bruised me and hurt my heart deeply with his strong personality, but God gave him the grace to grow in tenderness and patience. James recognized my weakness and encouraged me to verbalize everything I was already saying with my pouty face and posture. All my frustrations needed to come out verbally in conversation.

Mutually satisfying and peaceful resolution is always the goal of confrontation.

I didn't get there right away, but seeing James honor and validate my thoughts and opinions, even when we disagreed, helped me immensely in this critically important area. I began to realize what was going on inside my heart when I wasn't telling James how I felt about things, and we began to look at dealing with it as a necessary relationship builder. It was, and still is, one of the greatest things we've ever done for our marriage.

REACHING RESOLUTION

✦ JAMES

Betty and I want to make it abundantly clear that when we speak of confrontation, we aren't giving you license to tell off your spouse. Not in the slightest. We think of confrontation as simply laying our feelings on the table. It's saying in effect, "This is what I think, or this is what I feel. Now how do we look past our differences, hurts, and concerns and come to a positive resolution?"

Mutually satisfying and peaceful resolution is always the goal of confrontation. If you don't have this in mind when you're in the midst of conflict, you need to stop whatever you're doing and refocus your mind on the real aim of your discussion.

This is where our bedrock Scripture about not letting the sun go down on our anger comes into play. Every sunset is a conclusion, and every sunrise is a new beginning. This is exactly what you want in your relationship: you want a conclusion to whatever situation you're struggling through, and after you've achieved this conclusion, you want to leave the past behind you and live in a new beginning. You want a fresh start.

When Jesus taught us to pray, "Forgive us…as we have forgiven," He established a principle that so often applies to confrontation.[2] Matthew 18 teaches us about the futility of trying to worship God when we have unforgiveness in our hearts toward another person. Think how important this is when relating to your spouse.

To understand what Betty and I are referring to as conflict resolution, heavy emphasis must be placed on the word *resolution.* I have found that many couples with points of contention or conflict receive counsel that is not helpful. Many are finding conflict insulation rather than resolution. By that I mean they are finding someone to comfort them in their pain, and often this is someone who identifies with them because they have experienced or continue to experience similar painful conflicts themselves. This false sense of comfort will actually insulate a person from much-needed help.

So when we talk about resolution, we are describing coming to a point of understanding or agreement that may not necessarily do away with differences of opinion, various interests, or pastimes, but it will keep those interests from becoming a focal point at the expense of your spouse.

How do you know when you've achieved resolution? By studying *actions, attitudes,* and *atmosphere.*

In the midst of a disagreement, *actions* are a big clue to the way a person is thinking or feeling. Again, this highlights the importance of nonverbal communication. Your posture and the look on your face will give you away every time. If you can't look your spouse in the eye while you're confronting or being confronted, then you haven't made real progress. If you're sitting with your arms folded and your lips pursed, you're silently communicating that your spouse is blocked out of your personal space.

On the other hand, if you're leaning forward and making eye contact, you're indicating a desire for resolution. If you're reaching out to take your spouse's hand, and your spouse takes yours in return, then by your actions you're communicating to each other that your time of conflict is ending and resolution is on the way. After these serious times, we almost always put our arms around each other and hold each other tight, seeking a sense of peace.

Attitude is another key element in determining resolution. What is your attitude toward your spouse? What is your spouse's attitude toward you? You might be saying the right words and offering the right solutions, but are you doing it with the right attitude? Are you embracing your spouse with genuine forgiveness, or are you doing it begrudgingly? Are you offering a conciliatory hand out of love or out of obligation?

You must align your attitude with the characteristics of love. If you don't know the type of attitude you need to have, I recommend that you focus on Philippians 4:8: "Fix your thoughts on what is true, and honorable, and right, and pure, and lovely, and admirable. Think about things that are excellent and worthy of praise." Doesn't this sound like the type of attitude you should have toward your spouse?

Finally, determine the spiritual *atmosphere* in your relationship. What is the overall spirit in your home? After you've said your apologies and worked toward resolution, if you still feel a tension between you and your spouse, don't be afraid to mention it. Even a statement as simple as "I don't understand it, but I still feel as if something is wrong between us" is a good way to test the atmosphere and the spirit in your relationship.

If something is lingering in the atmosphere—such as a lack of peace—discuss that concern. If neither of you can identify it, pray and ask the Lord to guide you. You may need to spend time reconnecting in prayer in order to fully clear the air of tension, strife, or discord. An atmosphere of peace will prevail in a household or relationship when God's presence is welcomed.

God never fails. So when you lovingly confront your spouse, you can be certain that God will see you through your momentary discomfort, and you will witness the positive effect on your relationship. Words are never meaningless, and they do have an effect on the person speaking and the person hearing them. They can be a sharp sword or a healing balm.

Let it be forever settled between you and your spouse: agree that you will communicate and that you will confront because you love each other.

FOR REFLECTION AND DISCUSSION

Why is confrontation so difficult in a relationship?

Why is confrontation so important in marriage?

What tends to hinder the resolution of conflicts you have with your spouse?

10

Confession

This is the path to experiencing

shared mercy and grace.

JAMES

*A*s active participants in a fast-paced and information-saturated society, we all have a lot on our minds. We often have rapid-fire thoughts that come to us faster than we can process them, let alone say them out loud. Because of this, we are accustomed to keeping much of our internal monologue to ourselves.

That's fine, up to a point, but there comes a time when this hoarding of our thoughts can turn to resentment or lead to lustful thinking. That's when confession becomes necessary and helpful.

Don't misunderstand. Although the Bible instructs us to "capture...rebellious thoughts and teach them to obey Christ" (2 Corinthians 10:5), I'm not saying you have to publicly or openly confess every wayward thought that strays across your mind. Instead, I'm suggesting that whenever your thoughts or actions would grievously hurt your spouse, you should confess them and deal with them openly and honestly.

If you think your actions are all that matters, think again. Jesus plainly tells us that our thoughts and intentions are equally important: "Anyone who even looks at a woman with lust has already committed adultery with her in his heart" (Matthew 5:28). You can commit serious sin without ever acting on your thoughts, because God is always looking at your heart, not just at your outward actions (see 1 Samuel 16:7). Again, I am not suggesting that you spout aloud everything that comes into your mind, but I do want you to understand how important the battlefield of the mind is, especially when it comes to your marriage. And appropriate confession keeps us honest.

SHORT-TERM PAIN FOR LONG-TERM GAIN

Betty and I often take our dachshund, Princess, out to the country, where she loves to chase after small animals. Many times, as Princess hunts and sniffs around on the ground, she will start to limp and raise up one of her paws. It's a sad sight and always touches my heart. As soon as I can get to her, I pick her up to determine the cause of the pain. It's usually easy to find. Here in Texas we have a type of sandbur we call a sticker, a small brown sphere with many tiny, sharp spikes protruding from it. Often, one of these has lodged in Princess's paw, causing her pain.

When I find a sticker in Princess's paw, I know it needs to come out, since leaving it in would cause her to be hobbled. But I also know it will hurt her when I pull it out. In fact, it might hurt even more coming out than it did going in. So I have a choice. I can either leave the sticker in Princess's paw and let her hobble around in pain, or I can cause her more pain temporarily but ultimately improve her ability to run and play. To me the right choice is obvious: I pull out the sticker. Princess yelps at the pain, but soon she's back on the ground, running normally, chasing whatever she can find.

We all have stickers in our lives. Whether it's an addiction, an attitude, a habit, a past pain, or a current problem, it's something that is hurting us and preventing us from walking in freedom and unity in our relationships. Confession is the act of revealing our stickers to another person and saying, "Would you help me get this out of my life?"

Unfortunately, many people wind up just living with their stickers, afraid of the consequences if they confess. Princess doesn't try to get a sticker in her paw; it just happens while she's living her life. Yet it's easy for us to treat people's stickers as simply the consequences of their foolishness. Our attitude can be, "How did you get that problem? Shame on you! Why did you do that? You know better! What's wrong with you?" Not many people respond well to such a harsh, shame-on-you approach.

You must learn to welcome confession in each other.

If, as husband and wife, you can remember that you're a team, then you're going to do well when it comes time to remove stickers, whatever they are and however they got there. You must learn to welcome confession in each other, whether it's about anger, resentment, depression, bitterness, addiction, jealousy, lust, or whatever. It may be difficult initially to know, for example, that your spouse is disillusioned or depressed or downtrodden, but the Scriptures encourage us to lift each other up:

> Dear brothers and sisters, if another believer is overcome by some sin,
> you who are godly should gently and humbly help that person back
> onto the right path. And be careful not to fall into the same temptation
> yourself. Share each other's burdens, and in this way obey the law of
> Christ. If you think you are too important to help someone, you are
> only fooling yourself. You are not that important.[1]

These are strong words, but they're true. If, as followers of Christ, we are encouraged to "share each other's burdens," how much more should we do this in a marriage relationship? We should want to help all people who are defeated or hurting, but what person should we be more anxious to help than our own spouse?

Focus together on the problem, challenge, or weakness. Jesus promises that if two agree and are in harmony with God, they will discover what they are seeking.[2] If you will share your spouse's burdens, you will bring healing, strength, and confidence to your marriage.

FINDING A SAFE PLACE FOR CONFESSION

✦ BETTY

When we're struggling with feelings, thoughts, or temptations, often we are afraid to talk to other people—especially our friends at church—about our shortcomings. That's not how it's supposed to be, but when we're bothered by sin, we can wind up feeling ashamed and afraid to reveal the truth about ourselves. If we disclose our secrets, will others judge us harshly? Of course, "everyone has sinned; we all fall short of God's glorious standard" (Romans 3:23), but in those moments when we most need to confess, we can forget this central gospel truth and think we're the only person on earth struggling with sin and imperfections.

When it comes to marriage, though, a husband and wife already see most of each other's weaknesses and needs. The baggage can't be hidden. Your flaws, peculiarities, and imperfections will find their way to the surface, and your spouse has an unobstructed view. But your spouse also loves you too much to let those relatively minor things get in the way, and that's why he or she should be the safest person to confide in when you need to confess. That isn't always the case—I understand that—but I believe it's how God designed the marriage relationship to work, and such a place of refuge is what we should seek to establish in marriage. When your marriage is truly a safe haven, your spouse and you will both feel free to trust that God will change you just as much as He is changing your spouse.

Sometimes the closeness of the marriage relationship is a barrier to confession, because we don't want to disappoint, disillusion, or shock our closest companion. Sometimes a spouse is threatened by too much honesty. But when we try to hide ourselves within a marriage, or when we make our spouse feel as if he or she must hide in order to protect us from something, we actually undermine the integrity and strength of the relationship. Healing and restoration come when we're willing to be open and honest with each other.

When you realize that your mate already knows you're a broken, flawed vessel, you ought to be willing to lay everything on the table that requires confession and change so the two of you can acknowledge together the problems, focus on them, and then deal with them. Likewise, because you already know that your spouse has weaknesses, you can appreciate the need to provide a safe haven in which your spouse is free to openly and honestly confess his or her temptations, sins, and concerns without fear of reproach. One of the greatest gifts that a person can give his or her spouse is a feeling of safety and security, especially when it comes to confession.

> *Healing and restoration come when we're willing to be open and honest with each other.*

✦ JAMES

As we will discuss in detail in the next chapter, Betty gave me such a place of safety when I became so burned out in ministry and life that I didn't care whether I lived or died. I was able to tell her what was going on, and rather than shame me, she encouraged me to get the right kind of help. Because of her love, I didn't have to hide my true feelings. That's what an environment of confession promotes.

CONFESSION AND PRAYER

James 5:13–16 tells us how confession is not only for our own good but also for the good of those around us:

Are any of you suffering hardships? You should pray. Are any of you happy? You should sing praises. Are any of you sick? You should call for the elders of the church to come and pray over you, anointing you with oil in the name of the Lord. Such a prayer offered in faith will heal the sick, and the Lord will make you well. And if you have committed any sins, you will be forgiven. Confess your sins to each other and pray for each other so that you may be healed. The earnest prayer of a righteous person has great power and produces wonderful results.

Notice that we are encouraged to pray in addition to confessing our sins. Prayer releases God's forgiveness for our sins, but confession combined with prayer brings healing. Prayer is indeed a powerful tool that brings remarkable togetherness and unity to a marriage. Confession followed by prayer is a powerful tool for healing and restoration.

> *The Enemy will fight very hard to keep couples from praying together.*

Prayer is so powerful that the Enemy will fight very hard to keep couples from praying together. He knows that healing comes through prayer and through clear communication with each other. In fact, if there's one thing you and your spouse could do together that would pay off in every area of your lives—including your marriage—it would be to pray together every day.

According to Squire Rushnell and Louise DuArt (husband and wife) in their book *Couples Who Pray: The Most Intimate Act Between a Man and a Woman,* even "a very small investment [of praying together]—as little as five minutes a day—can deliver huge dividends for your marriage, drastically improving its course, and, as a result, changing your life."[3] Look at some of the evidence that Squire and Louise cite from a study conducted by Baylor University's Institute for Studies of Religion:

The following data provide the evidence—couples who pray sometimes versus those who pray a lot:

- 60% vs. 78% are likely to say their "marriage is happy"—a difference of 18%.
- 74% vs. 91% say, "My spouse is my best friend."
- 65% vs. 86% "try to make their marriage better"—a significant 21% distinction.
- 59% vs. 77% say, "My spouse makes me feel important."
- 52% vs. 72%—20% more—say the "quantity and quality of lovemaking is very good."
- 76% vs. 92% rate their confidence in the stability of their marriage as "very good."[4]

If you will take time to pray with your spouse, even if it's only for a few minutes each day, you will build trust and communicate a desire to improve your relationship. Prayer creates a special bond between a husband and wife and a pleasing climate for communication. Not only that, but prayer also invites God to take an active role in strengthening your marriage. You receive His guidance and direction, and prayer opens the conduit through which God can bring healing, forgiveness, and restoration. Prayer also helps to create a safe environment for confession to take place.

WHAT TO SAY?

✦ BETTY

When it comes to confession, ideally a husband and wife ought to be able to tell each other everything. James and I understand that few marriages are healthy enough to handle certain painful issues. Openness and honesty are certainly ideal, but some spouses may lack the spiritual maturity to handle them properly. Your marriage may not be ready for this now, but we encourage you to strive for complete openness and honesty in your relationship. It should be a constant pursuit, supported by both your actions and your words. "People who conceal their sins will not prosper, but if they confess and turn from them, they will receive mercy" (Proverbs 28:13).

James and I have worked hard to build trust so that we can feel safe when we need to confess to each other. After many years we reached a point where we knew we could talk openly without having to worry that the other person might slam-dunk us. We openly confess any sin or failure to each other, knowing that we will deal with the issue together in true oneness. When either of us misses the mark, the first place we go is to God and then to each other. I cannot emphasize this strongly enough: it is so important to air out things with each other and to pray for each other to be made whole in the relationship and for trust to remain strong.

If you keep your sins hidden, if you hold on to them, they will wind up holding you. As the Bible says, "His own iniquities will capture the wicked, and he will be held with the cords of his sin."[5]

But what if you don't have a solid relationship of trust and commitment with your spouse? What if your mate isn't a safe place for confession? How are you going to work toward this goal when you can't talk about your issues with your spouse?

If this is the case, James and I encourage you to look for a safe place within the church, a place where the leadership believes in the authority of Scripture and in lifting people up rather than putting them down. That is a place where you can find healing, where you can find someone to talk to. A wise, mature Christian counselor (whether it's a professional counselor or simply a mature Christian brother or sister) can help you deal constructively with your problems and communicate appropriately with your spouse.

If you go to someone other than your spouse, remember that you're there to focus on your life, not to complain about, accuse, or expose your spouse. You are confessing your own sins, not hers or his. If your spouse has failed, be careful to share that fact with concern and not a spirit of condemnation. If you want help, you can find it if you will swallow your pride, resist fear, and cry out for the freedom God offers.

Certainly, not every marriage is strong enough to handle immediately everything that you might feel the need to confess. This is why you must pray for wisdom, according to James 1:5: "If you need wisdom, ask our generous God, and he will give it to you." Once you have received wisdom, proceed with your God-led confession. You may not be able to unburden yourself completely, but that's the ultimate goal.

As we saw with the prophet Nathan in the story of David and Bathsheba, confession doesn't mean that you blurt out whatever you're thinking. You need to approach confession carefully, just as you would confrontation. Be honest with yourself and with your spouse. If you've sinned, don't shift the blame to the things that led you to the sin. Accept responsibility for your actions. But use your God-given wisdom to take care in what you say and the way you say it. God will guide you, and you will be healed.

THE KINDNESS OF CONFESSION

✦ JAMES

Instead of being a sign of failure, confession is one of the kindest things you can do for your spouse and yourself. It's an appeal for mercy and grace, both of which are rooted in kindness.

A good friend once told me one of the kindest, most merciful things I've ever heard about confession. "Repent while it's still a secret," he said. That's incredibly great advice! Since David kept his sin a secret and didn't confess or repent, his sin was exposed by the prophet Nathan. Moreover, David's failure to confess later brought serious consequences,

> *Confession is one of the kindest things you can do for your spouse and yourself.*

including the death of a son and public shame. God said through Nathan, "Out of your own household I am going to bring calamity upon you. Before your very eyes I will take your wives and give them to one who is close to you, and he will lie with your wives in broad daylight."[6]

Confession deals with sin according to God's invitation. When you confess, when you repent, you're acknowledging your responsibility instead of waiting to be found out. Confession is truly a marvelous thing!

Betty and I have seen many, many marriages in which a spouse was involved in some form of wrongdoing, but instead of confessing and repenting, he or she hid the sin until someone else exposed it. We've witnessed the horrendous pain that resulted. Of course healing is still available in such situations, but the consequences are so painful, particularly for innocent family members and friends.

Repent while it's still a secret.

Even worse, we have known many couples whose marriages were destroyed when a spouse's hidden sin was discovered. The lack of confession and repentance, on top of the sin itself, led to indescribable pain. It became too hard to forgive and to live with the shame. In most of these cases, often involving an extramarital affair, the result was doubly destructive: one person had the affair and was found out, the other person was hurt too deeply by it to forgive, and the marriage eventually dissolved.

Wouldn't it have been so much better for the person having the affair to repent before God and then confess to his or her spouse? Of course it would have been difficult, and the pain would have been real. But just like the sticker I removed from my dog's paw, the hurt would most likely have been temporary.

WHAT ABOUT SINS OF THE PAST?

How do you deal with something buried deep in your past? What if this involves some sin you engaged in long ago that you are now completely over?

Should you share those things with your spouse? What if you aren't married yet? Should you share the buried mistakes of your past with someone with whom you have a serious relationship? Should parents and grandparents tell children or grandchildren about past mistakes so they can learn from them?

These are questions to take to the Lord, seeking His wisdom. He will guide you. I believe there is a biblical principle that part of your power over the Enemy comes from your testimony (see Revelation 12:11), but that doesn't necessarily mean you have to air all your dirty laundry in explicit detail. Unbridled confession can feed gossip. Ultimately, the amount of detail you share when confessing your sins or giving your testimony is a question for God and family. If you believe there are things in your past that someone might reveal in the future, you may want to lay it out now. Confession is not for the purpose of satisfying someone's morbid curiosity or providing material for the tabloids.

It is important to remember that confession will make you feel better almost immediately, but you may not get better. You confess to each other in order to be healed, to be made whole. The purpose is to get well, and it is important that you do not seek simply comfort but that you commit to complete the journey toward wholeness. A doctor can give you medication or a pharmaceutical to help you feel better, but if he fails to get at the root of the problem, your disease may never be cured. Through wise counsel, we seek positive progress with our whole heart.

In the end, confession is necessary in order to live in wholeness, which is something we all should seek. Betty and I have agreed that we want to race Jesus to the side of the fallen and the hurting, even though we know He'll get there first, offering forgiveness and hope. When one of us stumbles, we are committed to lift each other up and to always provide a safe and secure place for confession. We practice this in our marriage, and we hope to extend the same grace in all our other relationships as well.

When you see your spouse in need, be quick to lift him or her up, no matter what. When you have a need to unburden yourself and confess, trust your spouse's heart to hear you. If your spouse can't handle that level of honesty, you may need to get some outside help. It may take time to reach the point where you can share openly, but you should diligently try to get there. You will experience great peace and security whenever you reach this place in your relationship.

HONESTY'S THE BEST POLICY

✦ BETTY

Both spouses should be honest with each other about what is going on in their lives. For one thing, it's a safeguard against having your spouse look outside the marriage for an interested or compassionate listening ear. This is especially important for husbands. They must have the freedom to confide in their wives about their lusts, ambitions, and desires without rocking the foundations of their marriage.

I know this isn't easy for most wives. It wasn't easy for me either. James has always been so open with me, but when he would come home after several weeks on the road and tell me about his struggles and temptations, I often felt threatened and insecure. I have always felt fortunate to have James as my husband, so the thought of other women being attracted to him—for all the same reasons I was—made me feel vulnerable and insignificant, especially when he was away from home. I loved what he was doing, and I thought it was wonderful how God had transformed his life and was using him. But I felt as if my own life didn't measure up and never would. I put expectations on myself and always came up short in my own eyes.

> *Husbands must have the freedom to confide in their wives about their lusts.*

I would look at the wives of other ministers and think, Oh, they're so gifted. They can get up and speak. They can sing or play a musical instrument. They have everything organized. They have so many gifts. What do I have? I didn't think I had any gifts. All I knew was that I wanted to be a dedicated wife and mother, which at the time—according to the prevailing wisdom in our society—didn't seem to be very important. You often heard, "I'm just a mother," or, "I'm just a housewife."

All those factors helped build jealousy in my life and made me feel insignificant and insecure. None of that was James's fault, though, because he would tell me how much he loved me, and he would encourage me in these areas. But until I overcame my performance-based faith—trying to do all the right things and keep up all the right appearances—and found my true identity in a growing relationship with God, James could tell me he loved me all day long, and it wouldn't lighten the load I was putting on myself. Until I learned to find my security in God's faithfulness, love, wisdom, and strength, there was nothing James could do to reassure me that his honesty about his struggles was not a danger signal.

It took me a long time to realize that when James acknowledged his weaknesses or battles, he was actually establishing a safety net. By being open about his struggles and temptations, he was including me in his life and helping to create accountability and trust. His confessions were not so much an indication that he was about to fall but rather that he was determined not to fall and that he needed my love and support to help him stand firm.

✦ JAMES

Another thing that fueled Betty's insecurity was the amount of time I was away from home. When I became successful very quickly in ministry, which happened around the same time we got married, the demands on my time multiplied exponentially. Whenever someone would say, "You have to come here because we need your help," I was too foolish to say no, and I spent way too much time away from Betty and my family.

A lot of people who become overcommitted to their work and their businesses believe they're doing it for their family, and they probably are in their heart. But when they get too busy to have time for their wife and children or to be sensitive to their family's needs, they end up destroying the very family they say they're working for. Others become consumed by success and lose sight of what's truly important in life. My busy schedule not only robbed my family of much-needed time with me; it also robbed me of very necessary time to be alone with God.

If you've wandered away from your spouse and family in your heart and mind, it's a good time to begin with confession. Admit that you've been distracted, and recommit yourself to your relationship. It's only when you're honest enough with yourself to admit you've done something wrong, and honest enough to confess your sins to God and to your spouse, that the process of confession, forgiveness, and reconciliation can begin.

 FOR REFLECTION AND DISCUSSION

Why is confession an important part of communication in marriage?

Why is it both easy and hard to confess something to your spouse?

Why is prayer so beneficial to a marriage?

11

Counsel

Everyone needs another's wisdom sometime.

BETTY

*A*bout fifteen years into our marriage, James and I found ourselves caught up in a vicious cycle that lasted for several years.

James began his ministry at age eighteen, and after nearly two decades of preaching five or six times a day for more than 250 days a year, he was no longer happy. He was burned out and exhausted, and as a result he became depressed and angry. He also acknowledged a serious battle with lust.

My attempts to help him only triggered my old fears and insecurities about being an inadequate partner for him in ministry. When he traveled, I was lonely and missed him. But when he was home, his dark moods and lack of joy made him difficult to be around. When he confessed his lustful thoughts and compulsive feelings, I felt helpless to respond. I kept asking him if I was doing something wrong, but he always assured me that it wasn't my fault. Still, I felt overwhelmed and incapable of being the kind of wife he needed. How could I be strong and help James when I was struggling so much myself?

I prayed for James, asking God to bring back the joy we'd had earlier in our marriage. Eventually it became clear that we needed outside help and counsel. When James returned from a trip and confessed that he had become so depressed and discouraged that he had considered deliberately crashing the plane he was flying, which would have killed not only him but a very good friend, we knew we had reached the breaking point. The next day James spent several hours talking with various friends, and when he was done, he told me he wanted to meet privately with a pastor from Florida, Peter Lord, who had spoken at our annual Bible conference. "I know I can trust Peter to keep things confidential," James said.

I encouraged him to meet with Peter as soon as possible, and James found the time while he was conducting a crusade in Miami. When he returned home, I could tell right away that something was different. James seemed at peace for the first time in a long time, and his hunger for the Word of God and his enthusiasm for preaching had returned. Always quick to tell me what was happening in his life, James explained how Peter had opened his eyes to the realities of spiritual warfare, especially how deceptive evil spirits could influence and oppress us—even as Christians.

At first I was confused. "I thought the devil and demonic spirits couldn't trouble us once we have Jesus in our hearts," I said.

"No, that's untrue," James replied. "And that's what Peter showed me. He gave me some references from Scripture to see for myself."

We'll discuss spiritual warfare in chapter 15, but for now I'll say that this timely counsel profoundly affected James. It was obvious that he had a new-found freedom. Sadly, that freedom didn't last.

When James shared what he had learned with some of his more conservative friends, including several prominent pastors, they scoffed and downplayed the role of evil spirits in affecting believers. James was troubled by their mocking response, but because he respected their knowledge of Scripture and their Christian maturity, he backed away from the teaching he had received and stopped pursuing the breakthrough he had experienced and so greatly desired.

Tragically, the spiritual battle intensified, which is just what Jesus said would happen when a spirit is driven out but the house is not then occupied by God's Holy Spirit and abiding presence. The Lord said that seven more spirits would come into the house and the condition would be far worse (see Matthew 12:43–45).

It wasn't until months later, when James not only received further counsel from a friend but also an unmistakable deliverance through the prayers of a humble servant of God, that he was truly set free from the forces that had sought to derail his life and ministry.

The lesson we learned is this: if you reach a point in your marriage when outside counsel is needed, pray for God's guidance. Ask Him to direct you to the right person or people in whom to confide. As with anything in life, when we seek outside counsel, we must do so with discretion and discernment. Not everyone we might choose will give us the kind of godly counsel we need.

James and I both believe that when a person is defeated and caught in an addictive practice, that problem must be acknowledged and outside assistance accepted. Serious problems such as substance abuse, alcoholism, and sexual addiction usually require a process that leads to positive change. Do not be ashamed to admit your failures or weakness.

Wives, although it may be difficult, if you discover problematic issues in your husband's life, I urge you not to write him off, throw him out, or give up on your marriage. Help is available and necessary.

NO MARRIAGE IS AN ISLAND

✦ JAMES

As we've seen thus far, commitment, trust, and communication are three pillars of a strong marriage. Whenever your commitment and trust are challenged, it's always good to try to work things out with your spouse, to communicate fully as husband and wife. But what should you do when you find yourselves unable to come to an agreement on your own? What must you do when neither of you has the wisdom needed to find resolution? This is when you must seek wise spiritual counsel.

Going to someone for help is not a sign of failure. In fact, it is quite the contrary; seeking outside counsel is an indication of strength and wisdom in a marriage. Let's face it. God did not design us to go it alone. That's why He gave us mates and why He placed us in families and among friends. Remember, the church is designed to be a family.

Going to someone for help is not a sign of failure.

We cannot get away from the fact that, at some time in our lives, we're going to need help beyond ourselves. Proverbs 27:17 tells us as much: "As iron sharpens iron, so a friend sharpens a friend." Asking another person for help or wisdom is simply asking to be sharpened.

Your dependence on others began the moment a single cell divided into two in your mother's womb. For nine months you depended completely on your mother as you grew from the miracle of conception into a newborn baby. Even after you were born, you couldn't care for yourself; you depended on the love of your parents for your care. As a child, you became more independent but still needed your parents for guidance and help with walking, feeding yourself, personal hygiene, tying your shoelaces, and riding a bicycle.

Then you moved into a phase in which you learned to rely on counsel from people other than your parents. You had friends in the neighborhood and teachers at school and maybe at Sunday school. As you grew, you had guidance counselors, driving instructors, coaches, club sponsors, youth pastors, college professors, and other people who influenced your life or mentored you. Even if some of that influence was negative, it did not negate the importance of good examples and the need for wise counsel.

John Donne famously wrote, "No man is an island, entire of itself." There is an inherent futility in trying to live your life strictly for yourself, guided only by yourself. Herein lies the beauty of the marriage relationship: by striving for a healthy marriage, you give of yourself to your spouse, and your spouse gives to you.

But just as no individual should be an island, no relationship should be an island either. Jesus spent almost His entire ministry intentionally pouring Himself into twelve disciples who would then take His truth to the world. And as Jesus prepared to be crucified and taken up into heaven, He said that we needed an Advocate, the Holy Spirit, to be our helper:

If you love me, obey my commandments. And I will ask the Father, and he will give you another Advocate, who will never leave you. He is the Holy Spirit, who leads into all truth. (John 14:15–17)

When the Father sends the Advocate as my representative—that is, the Holy Spirit—he will teach you everything and will remind you of everything I have told you. (John 14:26)

But I will send you the Advocate—the Spirit of truth. He will come to you from the Father and will testify all about me. And you must also testify about me because you have been with me from the beginning of my ministry. (John 15:26–27)

But now I am going away to the one who sent me, and not one of you is asking where I am going. Instead, you grieve because of what I've told you. But in fact, it is best for you that I go away, because if I don't, the Advocate won't come. If I do go away, then I will send him to you. (John 16:5–7)

According to Jesus, it is necessary for us to rely on the Holy Spirit for guidance and help in life. The point is this: we have to rely on influences outside of ourselves. An occasion may arise when you will reach an impasse in your marriage relationship, when you realize you aren't hearing each other, and for whatever reason you're not able to hear the Holy Spirit clearly either. During these times you need to be willing to get outside help together.

Every Team Needs a Coach

No matter the sport, all great teams have a few things in common: they see the goal as greater than the individual, they work together to achieve this common goal, and they have a coach.

The coach is often the most important part of the team. Because the coach isn't on the playing field, the coach has a great sideline view of how the team's doing. Whereas the team is immersed in the action on the field, the coach is nearby and able to see both the positives and the negatives in the way the team is performing. This allows the coach to make adjustments that encourage the positives and correct the negatives.

According to Jesus, it is necessary for us to rely on the Holy Spirit for guidance and help in life.

In your marriage team, you have a coach. This coach is the Holy Spirit, your Advocate. He will guide you toward being the most effective team you can be, encouraging your positives and gently correcting your negatives.

Most head coaches have assistant coaches who help prepare and guide the team. Most assistant coaches focus on a specific aspect of the sport, such as offense or defense, strength training, conditioning, or other functions. Head coaches rely on their assistants to help them accomplish the goal: victory.

God also has assistant coaches—His followers—whom He has placed in the church as part of the fivefold ministry of the Spirit (see Ephesians 4:11–13). As God's followers and assistant coaches, we all have different jobs. Some of us are apostles; others are prophets; some are evangelists; others are pastors or teachers. Some of God's followers are equipped to handle a counseling role in your relationship.

Betty and I are big football fans. Imagine a quarterback who isn't being effective during a game. He isn't reading the defense well, and he keeps missing his receivers. He's not throwing the ball as accurately as he could. He isn't on the same page with his offensive line. He's just playing poorly. Whom on the coaching staff would he turn to? Would he go to the person in charge of the defense? Would he go to the person in charge of the kicking game? Of course not. He would go to the person in charge of the quarterbacks, the one person on the sideline who is focused on him.

In the same way, God, through the Holy Spirit, is your marriage's head coach, and He has placed assistant coaches in your life to help you in specific areas. If you're having a problem in your marriage, go to the proper coach. Take your challenges to someone who is uniquely qualified to help you get to where you need to be to achieve victory.

The Holy Spirit knows His coaching staff; He knows who you need to see in order to find healing in your relationship. He will guide you to that person. Ask the Holy Spirit for help, and watch Him put your relationship back in the winner's bracket. Don't lose hope. These wonderful helpers are available, and you can find them with the Spirit's help.

COUNSEL AND TEAMWORK

✦ BETTY

It is important to understand that the decision to seek outside counsel is not to be taken lightly; nor is it to be undertaken individually. When the need arises to go outside your marriage for help, you and your spouse must maintain your commitment to work together. James and I highly recommend that you make a joint decision to seek the help of a counselor.

Sometimes it can be helpful to seek advice from a professional who doesn't know you or your spouse. Look for a person with strong professional credentials and a faith-based approach. Many churches provide a list of referrals, or they may have a well-trained counselor on staff who is both qualified and caring.

You don't need to suffer in silence, and you don't need to cry out behind each other's backs. If you're in the midst of a difficult time and you can't see any way out, please let me encourage you: there *is* a way. Pray and ask God for His direction in finding help. If you ask Him for an egg, He won't give you a scorpion.[1] No, if you ask Him, He will give you the Holy Spirit, and the Holy Spirit will guide you into all truth.[2]

Most important, ask God to help you and your spouse remain united as a team. When you're upset with something your husband or wife has said or done, there is a huge temptation to seek a sympathetic ear. As the saying goes, "Misery loves company." We want to unload, telling all the ways we're right and our spouse is wrong. We want someone to be as upset as we are and to validate our feelings.

This is not a good idea. It's also not what we mean by seeking counsel. Commiserating with people just to get them on your side is merely stewing in your own juices and inviting others into the pot with you. It is treacherous because you run the risk of fostering an air of superiority over your spouse. If you continue to do this, you can eventually find yourself resenting your spouse rather than moving toward understanding and reconciliation.

Please be very careful when discussing your spouse's weaknesses without his or her consent, because it can result in deep feelings of betrayal.

Instead, take your concerns first to God, and then take them to your spouse. After you've prayed and spoken to your spouse, if you still have no resolution, take your concerns—together with your spouse—to someone you both agree on. James and I have never approached another person to discuss a challenge or difficulty in our marriage unless we have first addressed it between ourselves and then have explicitly agreed to discuss this particular challenge with a trusted friend or counselor. We never have and never will go behind each other's back. Believe me, this practice has enabled us to work through some very serious challenges.

It was essential for both James and me to seek and accept outside help. We needed someone we could trust when we shared information on recurring defeats in our lives. Thankfully, we found someone who would actually advise us, then would pray and take authority over the tormenting spirits of deception, distraction, fear, and rejection that had effectively held us in bondage. (Please read chapter 15 prayerfully.)

What if you just need someone to help you sort out your feelings? It's no secret that women and men see things differently, and occasionally you might want to bounce a few thoughts off someone other than your spouse to help you gain perspective. This is perfectly normal and fine as long as your spouse knows what you are doing and agrees to it. Of course there are occasions when outside counsel must be sought

Take your concerns first to God, and then take them to your spouse.

privately, as when a spouse has become physically abusive or dangerous in some other way. Otherwise it's usually best if both spouses agree on a course of action.

You don't ever want to get into a pattern of running to someone other than your spouse when there's a problem. It's all right to occasionally talk to a trusted friend or parent but only if this person understands his or her place in your relationship and doesn't try to usurp authority. We have a tendency to run to people who will side with us, but that can defeat the purpose of seeking outside counsel. It's typically much healthier to seek the counsel of a wise and impartial counselor, and that's why we encourage you to seek outside counsel together. You need someone to help you resolve your differences; you don't need someone to build your case.

Also—and this should go without saying, but just to be clear—*never* talk about your marital challenges with someone of the opposite sex, even if he or she is a close friend. All too often this type of counsel leads to an inappropriate emotional relationship. How many pastors have fallen into sin as the result of a relationship that began as a counseling appointment? James and I have witnessed many situations like this that have blossomed into a full affair. If you must talk one-on-one to someone outside your marriage relationship, choose a trusted friend or counselor of the same sex who will understand the unique feelings and thoughts of your gender.

You can't expect to overcome your challenges instantly.

Another important thing to remember is that you can't expect to overcome your challenges instantly. It will take time for you and your spouse to work through the difficulties you're encountering, and you will likely need to seek outside counsel more than once.

Job's Friends and Unwanted Counsel

✦ James

There's a big difference between asking for help and getting unsolicited help. When you are in a challenging time in your relationship, there will always be people who will offer unsolicited opinions. With the help of your Advocate, the Holy Spirit, you must judge those opinions based on the Word of God.

In the Old Testament book of Job, we see an extended story of this type of meddling. God tested Job, and everything in Job's life was taken from him. His wealth, his children, his health—all of it was destroyed in an instant by Satan. Yet Job remained a faithful servant of God, trusting He would make all things right.

However, we are told in Job 2:11, "When three of Job's friends heard of the tragedy he had suffered, they got together and traveled from their homes to comfort and console him." This was all well and good, and I'm sure the gesture was appreciated. But for the next thirty-five chapters of the book, Job's friends give him nothing but bad advice and offer an unwanted exposition of their thoughts concerning both his failure and God's. They came to console Job, but instead they misrepresented the truth and told him things he didn't need to hear.

Unfortunately, our gossip-obsessed culture is full of people like Job's friends. They are happy to offer their opinions—no matter how wrongheaded—about how we should act, think, and feel. No doubt the consolation offered by Job's friends came from an equal mixture of genuine concern and feelings of superiority. After all, they weren't going through Job's painful trial.

Many well-intentioned do-gooders will look at the challenges in your marriage and offer opinions about how you should proceed. Sometimes these opinions will be correct; many times they will be incorrect, unbiblical, and unhelpful. This is when you need to diligently seek the Lord for guidance. Check your friends' advice against what you read in the Bible. Do their words line up with the words of God as recorded in Scripture? Do they bring peace to your heart? If you can answer yes to both questions, then their advice is worthy of consideration. The New Testament Christians were exhorted to examine "the Scriptures daily to see whether these things were so."[3]

On the other hand, if this unsolicited advice doesn't make sense in light of Scripture and if it only brings turmoil to your heart, then most likely it isn't something you need to consider. As we saw in the story of King David and the prophet Nathan, God often uses people to speak to us when we aren't expecting it, so we need to be able to discern these times. If someone's words only bring strife and turmoil to our lives, and if they don't ring true with the Bible, then we need to put them aside and diligently search for true, godly counsel.

Check your friends' advice against what you read in the Bible.

Jesus said, "Keep on seeking, and you will find."[4] God is more anxious to guide us, comfort us, and provide counsel than we can ever comprehend.

All in all, we believe it's best for you to keep your commitment to God, to each other, and to the teamwork of your relationship by agreeing together to seek counsel as a couple and to let God change you through the words and work of the counselor.

FOR REFLECTION AND DISCUSSION

Why should a marriage not be "an island, entire of itself"?

Why is seeking help from an outside source for a marriage challenge not a sign of failure?

Most of the time, why is it a good idea to discuss a difficult relationship issue with your spouse before talking to someone on the outside?

PART 4

Challenges

12

Money

Pursue the true wealth that lasts.

JAMES

*E*very marriage will inevitably face challenges along the way. The question is not "Will our marriage face challenges?" but "When challenges come, how effectively will we deal with them?"

Up to now we've talked about a number of marriage principles. How do we apply them in real-life situations? It's one thing to understand the importance of commitment, trust, and communication, but the rubber meets the road when these principles are tested by our circumstances and experiences.

In the next several chapters, we'll look at some challenges that every couple faces in marriage. Based on a lot of hard-knocks experience, we can offer practical advice on facing these issues. In addition, we're happy to refer you to other authors and experts who can provide more specific instruction on how to manage these challenges of married life.

One of the first and most important issues that every couple must agree on is how to manage their finances. Aside from poor communication and infidelity, financial problems are perhaps the most common factor in marriages that are on the road to ruin. What sorts of practical methods can you employ to avoid the pitfalls of financial problems and the devastation they can cause in your marriage?

LIVE WITHIN YOUR MEANS

✦ BETTY

Right from the start, James and I came to a crucial agreement, one we believe is supported by the words of the Bible. We agreed not to indulge in compulsive spending and not to try to impress people with any of the stuff we had. As James likes to say, "It's okay to have stuff; it's not okay for stuff to have you." Never allow the things you possess to possess you.

The Bible tells us plainly in Philippians 2:3–4, "Don't be selfish; don't try to impress others. Be humble, thinking of others as better than yourselves. Don't

Self-gratifying spending never satisfies.

look out only for your own interests, but take an interest in others, too." There simply isn't room in the Christian life to worry about impressing other people. We should never want something because someone else has it or because it's a status symbol. There's nothing wrong with possessing the things you need or even the things you want. But how can you "take an interest in others" if you're drowning in debt?

Paul also tells us in Philippians that God will supply our needs.[1] And he says in 2 Corinthians that if we learn to keep God first, even in our giving, He will enable us to give to every good work.[2] In the book of Proverbs, we are told, "Honor the LORD with your possessions, and with the firstfruits of all your increase" (3:9, NKJV). When we keep God first, it's amazing how much better we manage our money.

The part of you that wants to impress people and to revel in vanity—the part that wants to determine your personal worth based on your possessions—is the part that has to die. You will never be happy if you try to base who you are on what you have. This way of thinking leads only to dissatisfaction and a constant pursuit of "uncertain riches."[3] When you build your self-worth on the foundation of money, you're foolishly building your house on an unstable foundation.[4]

Self-gratifying spending never satisfies. Living for earthly treasures and pleasures leads to a slow form of death. As Ecclesiastes 5:10 tells us, "Those who love money will never have enough. How meaningless to think that wealth brings true happiness!" This was written by King Solomon, one of the wisest and wealthiest men who ever lived. He was speaking from experience, having discovered in his old age that money and possessions didn't satisfy him.

If you're currently pursuing or living for foolish material gain, we encourage you to take these thoughts and attitudes to the Lord and to start living under His control, not out of control. God wants the best for you, but His best often looks much different from what the world thinks is best.

> *Find your worth in God, and you'll experience true prosperity.*

Find your worth in God, and you'll experience true prosperity. Jesus promises us an abundance of life, which is not the same as an abundance of possessions. If, however, you keep first things first, you can and will enjoy all things richly.[5]

✦ JAMES

Betty and I are not financial experts by any means, but over the past fifty years, we have made some financial decisions that have proven wise. Very early on we decided we would try to be as prudent as possible with our money, mainly because we had very little of it. We determined not to spend what we didn't have, and we decided to live not just at our means, but *below* our means. That may sound impossible, but believe me, it's not—even today.

For us it meant not using credit for anything we considered nonessential, such as a television, dishwasher, or washer and dryer. We considered a refrigerator a necessity, and we bought one we could afford. If we wanted an appliance or piece of furniture, we saved until we had enough money to pay cash for it. For any of the essentials, such as food and clothing, we always paid cash. And if we wrote a check, we first made sure the money was in our bank account. We never attempted to float a check, hoping to cover it before it was cashed.

Credit cards and easy credit were not as prevalent fifty years ago as they are today, but even when we received our first credit card, we didn't use it unless we knew we could pay the bill in full as soon as it arrived. The same is true today. Bank debit cards can be safe and effective—if used as a plastic check.

Debt can be an oppressive weight; if allowed to accumulate, it will eventually become so heavy, it can pull your marriage apart. Betty and I did everything we could to avoid debt, and we started with our home. When we were first married, we rented an apartment, which we felt was reasonable for a young couple. There's no sense in saddling a fledgling marriage with the responsibility of homeownership. In America we are currently witnessing the tragic consequences of easy-to-get subprime mortgages that couples and individuals could not afford.

We started in an apartment and then moved into a ten-foot-by-fifty-foot mobile home. By the time our eldest daughter, Rhonda, was about three years old, we had finally saved enough money for a 20 percent down payment and bought a home. Even then, we didn't overreach on the payments. We bought a modest home with a very small payment that was easy for us to make. Here's the bottom line—and wouldn't you love it today—we paid $2,000 down and $109 per month.

We were frugal with our money. We never felt an urge to keep up with the Joneses, and we were not infatuated with grownup toys. We didn't buy nonessentials. Instead, we lived modestly and never made any giant leaps into financial stress. If we had to ask ourselves, "Can we afford this?" we knew the answer was likely no. Our fiscal restraint eventually put us in a position to obtain things we never imagined we could have.

CREDIT CARDS AND COMPULSIVE SPENDING

✦ BETTY

James and I had to decide early in our marriage what type of financial lifestyle we were going to have. Because we had both grown up in families that didn't have much money, we knew it would take some solid financial thinking and good decisions to keep money from adversely affecting our marriage.

We determined to invest only in things that produced equity. If we had to borrow money, it needed to be for something—like a house—that we could turn around and sell for as much or more than we'd financed it for.

One of our biggest and best decisions concerned credit cards. These days credit cards can be useful for convenience, but they should never be used for short- or long-term credit. Pay them off each month, and you won't run into trouble. Credit cards possess a tragic downside, because they can easily change from a tool to a trap. It's far too easy to run up a huge bill, and before you know it, you're caught up in debt and making high-interest payments on things you shouldn't have bought in the first place. Credit card companies make promises that lure the unsuspecting into foolish spending, and then the companies almost secretly increase the interest rates.

When James and I finally started to use a credit card, we decided not to think of it as credit. Instead, we used it like a debit card—a plastic check. If we didn't have the money to pay for something, we would not put it on our credit card. We used our credit card only if we knew we had the money in the bank and could pay the bill when it came.

By using credit cards this way, we denied ourselves instant pleasures, but we were able to save enough money to get the furniture and appliances we wanted and to pay for them outright, which saved us an incredible amount of money in interest payments from the beginning of our marriage.

To this day we live below our means. But saving money on credit card interest has allowed us to raise our means, which in turn has raised our standard of living.

LIVING BELOW THE STRESS LEVEL

✦ JAMES

Betty and I have had many challenges in our marriage, but we thank God that financial stress has never threatened to tear us apart. Early in our life together, we made the crucial decision not to allow those stresses into our relationship.

Living below your means and making wise choices in spending your money are not decisions you make once and for all. Instead, they are daily and lifelong commitments, and they become more critical with each passing day, especially in our buy-now, pay-later culture.

Betty and I encourage every couple we counsel to deny the spending impulses encouraged by the world and their own selfish desires. There is an impulse that says happiness can be attained by purchasing stuff, an impulse that says you can't live without the latest gadget or even an older gadget you've already managed to live without for some time.

I don't want you to feel guilty about any recent purchases, and I believe that, most of the time, there's room for an occasional splurge. I am saying that you need to cultivate an attitude that says, "God, You alone are my source of happiness." Your finances are a reflection of your heart, and your financial decisions are heart decisions.

Jesus said in the Sermon on the Mount, "Where your treasure is, there your heart will be also."[6] When you make a purchase, are you making it out of necessity, or are you just hoping to fill a void in your life? I've known many people who, if they were honest with themselves, would have to admit it's the latter.

It's just human nature. Look at Psalm 119:36: "Give me an eagerness for your laws rather than a love for money!"

"A love for money" is a potential problem for all of us. Money is a powerful tool, and many of us make bad decisions because we are intoxicated by the power of money. Nevertheless, the desire for money is one we must control. Proverbs 11:28 states, "Trust in your money and down you go! But the godly flourish like leaves in spring."

Paul writes in 1 Timothy 6:9–10, "People who long to be rich fall into temptation and are trapped by many foolish and harmful desires that plunge them into ruin and destruction. For the love of money is the root of all kinds of evil. And some people, craving money, have wandered from the true faith and pierced themselves with many sorrows." He isn't saying that money itself is evil but that "the love of money is the root of all kinds of evil." Taking money out of its proper place and loving it and what it can do can lead to destruction.

Money itself is neither good nor bad. It is simply a tool we must use properly and responsibly. In the same way that a chainsaw can either cut a limb off a tree or cut off somebody's arm, money used incorrectly can do great damage to ourselves and to our marriage. If we use it the way God intends, we can accomplish many positive things.

Betty and I took seriously God's Word when it says to honor Him with the "firstfruits of all [our] increase" (Proverbs 3:9, NKJV). We believe that giving tithes and offerings is an indicator of where our hearts are and what is in first place in our lives.

> *Money itself is neither good nor bad.*

We also found a lot of safety and security by living within our budget. Most of the items on our budget are fixed or predictable amounts, such as our house payment and utilities. The expenses that aren't fixed are ones we agreed on long ago, such as how much we want to save and how much we're willing to spend on dining out, entertainment, and those types of things.

When it comes to finances in marriage, you must fall back on your prior commitment to God. He must be first and foremost in your life, and He must be your source of contentment and peace of mind. You cannot look to your spouse, your children, your possessions, or your career to provide happiness—none of those things will provide lasting happiness. Instead, all of them in some way, at some time, will disappoint you.

Make a firm decision now to build your financial future on the solid rock of your commitment to God. Once you've done this, make another firm decision together—to live below your means. Americans in general are terrible at living below their means. Many have foregone saving money in order to spend it—often very foolishly. I know far too many people who barely make it from paycheck to paycheck.

I strongly encourage you to get your financial house in order. Begin to make wise decisions and commitments now, even if you've never done it before. You have a general idea of the amount of money you make in a month or in a year. Determine how you're going to spend it, and make it intentional. Do it together with your spouse, and you will greatly strengthen and stabilize your relationship. Do it according to Scripture, and you will confirm your commitment to God. Discuss everything thoroughly with your spouse, and you will enhance your communication skills. Determine to live free from the bondage that will surely come if your finances are not under control.

If you need help with specific strategies, we recommend the writings of Dave Ramsey, Ron Blue, Larry Burkett, Howard Dayton, and Randy Alcorn.[7] If your finances are a problem area in your marriage, seek wise outside counsel for ways to deal with your debt and establish a workable budget. Get your financial challenges figured out, and you will greatly strengthen and enhance your marriage.

There is nothing wrong with considering and even dreaming about future financial possibilities. Your dreams do matter, as long as you don't allow them to become idols that lead to foolish spending.

Shortly after Betty and I married, we discussed how much fun it would be if our family had a place by a lake or near wildlife. We thought a getaway could be very special to all of us. As a result of these dreams, we bought furniture for our first apartment that we thought would look great in a cabin. Many years later we had just such a place and already owned the furniture.

If you live wisely and frugally, you can live your dreams. It's never too late to put first things first and set your financial house in order. We all have dreams, and rightly so. But I suggest that you lay them at the feet of Jesus and, in so doing, leave them in the hands of God. Do not put them on the altar of endless pursuit, allowing them to become an idol. When we trust our heart's desire to God, keeping Him first, it is amazing to watch Him grant us our heart's desire, because He is our delight.

FOR REFLECTION AND DISCUSSION

Why does money cause so much conflict for couples?

What are the critical money challenges in your marriage?

What changes will need to occur for your spouse and you to live within your means?

13

Parenting

It takes a good team to rear a child.

JAMES

Other than marriage itself, I believe parenting is the greatest responsibility you can take on in your life. As with marriage, achieving success with this challenge is one of the most rewarding accomplishments you will ever experience. As Betty and I have watched our children grow and become parents themselves, our hearts have overflowed with love and admiration. And now we see our grandchildren also making good, godly choices. However, standing near the end of our time as parents and looking back is much easier than being on the other side—just starting out and discovering the many twists and turns on the road called *parenting*.

One of the first decisions Betty and I made had to do with our commitment to teamwork. We knew we had to face our role as parents together, because parenting, as we discovered, is a 100 percent team effort. For kids, most of childhood is an exploration of boundaries, of seeing which foundations are firm and which foundations will crumble when limits are challenged. If children see that their parents aren't on the same page, they instinctively test the boundaries to see how far their parents will let them go. They also test to see if mom and dad are standing together or if they can be pitted against each other. If one parent is a softer touch, the children figure this out and will constantly go to the more lenient parent, which causes tension between mom and dad.

Parenting, as we discovered, is a 100 percent team effort.

Children don't set out to act this way; it's a part of growing up. They explore their boundaries and sometimes push on the fence to see if it will fall. This is why, as parents, we must be rock solid in our determination to stick together, even if we don't agree on every point.

Betty and I may have differed on a few specifics, such as how we administered discipline or correction, but we always supported each other and didn't bring our disagreements into the equation unless we could share some valuable lesson by explaining our different perspectives on a matter. Our children learned very early that they could not pit one of us against the other, and I believe this created a strong foundation of security, love, and respect.

LOVE FOR EACH OTHER

When you commit to oneness in parenting, you're recommitting yourself to live in love, and there is no greater gift you can give your children than the deep-rooted knowledge that their mom and dad really love each other. When your children see this, when they see their father loving their mother the way she deserves to be loved, and they see their mother loving and respecting their father in the same way, they are exposed to a powerful truth. They're exposed to the gospel in action and witness a visible demonstration of its power.

The Bible says Jesus will love us no matter what—even against the logic of what we deserve. Jesus gave His all for us, and there is nothing we can do to erase His love. When husbands, wives, fathers, and mothers display this same love to each other, they're also showing it to their children. Indirectly we are saying to them, "Just as I love your mother (or father) without any reservation, that same love is there for you."

Because your kids are watching the way you relate to each other, especially when conflict arises, you must be diligent to preserve your "unity...in the bond of peace."[1] Children are smart and intuitive, and they can tell when something's wrong. In those instances, the worst thing you can do is turn to them for counsel or unburden yourself to them. They are too young to help you process your feelings, and they don't need to become an advisor for you. They need to lean on you; you don't need to lean on them.

In those inevitable times when conflict arises between you and your spouse, and your children witness your heated discussions, you're actually doing them a great favor by allowing them to see how you work out your differences by applying the principles of commitment, trust, and communication. In order to succeed in life, your kids need to learn the proper way to resolve conflict. When they see you and your spouse working through your tensions together, keeping your communication open, honest, respectful, and flowing—and seeing you both admit when you've been wrong—they will have the right model to guide them in their future relationships. You can and should acknowledge your failures and let them see your willingness to change.

I don't want you to mistakenly think I'm giving you carte blanche to start arguing in front of your children. I am telling you it's okay for your kids to see the process of conflict and resolution, as long as they see the complete process and as long as conflict is not the normal state of your home. If children never see their parents confront each other and then have meaningful conflict resolution, the kids will have missed a wonderful learning opportunity.

> *It's okay for your kids to see the process of conflict and resolution, as long as they see the complete process.*

Some people believe that children should never see their parents argue. The fact is that healthy relationships often have peaks and valleys. Passionate people usually have opinions about matters of importance. If couples never argue, it makes you wonder about the passion in their marriage. We realize that some people are even keeled and may not be inclined to argue their points. But please realize that apathy can be negative for children to absorb, and it does not demonstrate healthy conflict resolution.

It all comes back to teamwork. You and your spouse are in your relationship together, and this crucial dimension doesn't change when it comes to parenting. You are parents together as well, and you need to rely on each other in all the parental tasks. Once your children realize you are an unshakable team, they will relax and respond, knowing they're in a safe place.

THE IMPORTANCE OF BOUNDARIES

✦ BETTY

Boundaries are such a vital part of the instructional time you have with your children, because you are training them to become adults. You aren't raising children; you're rearing future adults. They need to learn right from wrong early in their lives.

When your children are young, you have to place boundaries around them to keep them safe and make them feel secure. For example, let's say you send your children outside to play in the yard. You may put up a fence to keep them out of the street, and you may tell them, "Stay in the backyard." But it's good to take this a step further and let your children know why the boundary—the restriction—exists. You explain that it's best—not only for you, but also for them. The curiosity to explore and push boundaries makes it necessary to have gates and locks on fences they can't climb. You benefit from having the kids stay in the yard, because you can just look out the window and check on them, and you'll have peace of mind in knowing they aren't being exposed to traffic. But they need to understand the benefit for them as well: you want them to stay in the yard because it's much safer than playing in the street. You aren't restricting them for your own reputation, image, or desire. You're restricting them for their safety and well-being. A fence is a line of protection, a source of security, not a prison wall.

This principle of boundaries has its parallels in how we view God's Word. Many people see the laws and edicts of the Bible as a form of bondage or imprisonment, but the boundaries God has placed on us in Scripture are actually there for our protection. They aren't intended to enclose us or fence us in; they're intended to show us the way to true freedom—freedom from living for ourselves. Neither God nor loving parents are trying to limit life, liberty, and joy. Both are seeking to extend and enhance them.

You aren't raising children; you're rearing future adults.

> If you obey all the decrees and commands I am giving you today, all will
> be well with you and your children. I am giving you these instructions so
> you will enjoy a long life in the land the LORD your God is giving you
> for all time. (Deuteronomy 4:40)

> Oh, that they would always have hearts like this, that they might fear
> me and obey all my commands! If they did, they and their descendants
> would prosper forever. (Deuteronomy 5:29)

> Be careful to obey all the commands I am giving you today. Then you
> will live and multiply, and you will enter and occupy the land the LORD
> swore to give your ancestors. (Deuteronomy 8:1)

In the same way, the boundaries you give your children as they grow up are really there to establish and preserve their freedom. If you instill the correct principles in them when they're young, as they get older, they won't need a fence around the yard to keep them from playing in the street. This may sound simplistic, but it's actually a powerful principle that will guide your children throughout their lives.

TELLING, TEACHING, AND TRAINING

✦ JAMES

In preparing your children for adulthood, there are three basic ways to instruct: *telling*, *teaching*, and *training*. These may sound similar, but they are not the same thing. Training is far superior to the other two.

In elementary school, or even in preschool, teachers typically have a time called show and tell. Parents must understand the importance of *tell and show*. If you only tell your children what to do, you leave them on their own to figure out how, which can lead to resentment and feelings of insecurity. You can tell your children to pray, for example, but if you aren't doing it yourself, if you're not modeling the right behavior, what you say is nothing more than empty words.

Likewise, you can teach your children, which is a step beyond just telling them, but it still doesn't go far enough. Teaching involves offering your children instruction on a certain way to live and maybe providing the reasons why, but it stops short of giving them opportunities to practice what they've learned. Using the same example of prayer, you might teach your kids how to pray by having them listen to you pray. It's good for them to see you do it, but it leaves them as spectators. If you don't take the instruction to the next level—by allowing them to practice prayer on their own—you leave them with knowledge but no experience.

Sadly, a lot of parenting we've observed over the years stops at the level of teaching. The kids grow up with their heads full of rules and regulations and things they've seen their parents do, but they've never been allowed to test the rules or the boundaries and make them their own.

No doubt, at one time or another, you've heard Proverbs 22:6 quoted in connection with parenting: "Train up a child in the way he should go, even when he is old he will not depart from it" (NASB). But what does it mean to "train up a child in the way he should go"?

Betty and I believe it has to do with understanding your children and understanding what they need to know in order to succeed as adults. Then you diligently instruct them in the proper ways to live, and you give them opportunities to practice, fail, learn, and grow as they get older. We also believe it means that, along with instruction, you seek to help them understand the reasons for doing things a certain way. Children should learn that there are negative consequences for bad decisions and actions. Sin leads to God's judgment.

It's not enough just to tell them or show them or even let them try it on their own. For training to have its greatest effect, we must also walk alongside our children and correct them, teaching them how to refine and internalize the instruction so it becomes a guiding principle in their lives, not merely a set of dos and don'ts. Training involves establishing boundaries and then allowing your kids to test their wings within the boundaries until they learn to fly freely, without veering off course.

Do you see the difference between training and merely telling or teaching? Perhaps an additional example will help.

Betty and I both love to watch football, and she really gets into the games. On the football field we see the difference between training and teaching and telling. Through repetitive drills, film study, and interactive instruction, a good coach trains his players how to block, tackle, run a good pass route, and set up in the pocket. If the coach only told his players what to do, they wouldn't last two minutes on game day. If he just taught them how to play football, they'd have a lot more information, but they would still struggle on the field, because they wouldn't have learned how to do what they were supposed to do.

> *For training to have its greatest effect, we must also walk alongside our children and correct them.*

That's why a good coach trains his players. He tells them what he wants them to do and teaches them how to do it, and then the players take their training onto the field and put into practice all they've learned. Coaches don't just tell players what to do; they show them. Coaches then watch as players try to do what they've been taught, and the coaches provide correction and further instruction. As players get better, their coaches begin to expect more from them. They teach them further levels of refinement until the process is fully trained into them by repetitive practice.

But even that's not enough. The players still must go onto the field on the weekend and perform in game situations against an opponent who is trying to undermine their efforts at every turn, attempting to defeat them.

Raising kids is very much like training football players. As coaches for our kids, we must train them for life. We must instruct them in the proper ways to live. We must give them hands-on demonstrations and model correct behavior and attitudes. We must set a good example and then give our kids room to work things out on their own. We must also watch how they respond and provide appropriate correction and further instruction.

All this is to prepare them for the day when they will fly from the nest and test their wings in the real world—a world in which they will face adversity and opposition from the schemes of Satan and from life itself. Give your children understanding and wisdom; they will thank you for it. Your marriage—and theirs—will be blessed because of it. When you watch them live out what they have learned through love and training, you will, as Peter said, experience "joy inexpressible and full of glory" (1 Peter 1:8, NASB).

MAKING A DIFFERENCE WITH DISCIPLINE

Although discipline has become controversial in our society, it is nonetheless an important part of the training process. Without it, the training process lacks the necessary corrective element to make it truly effective. Discipline is all about bringing, or allowing, appropriate consequences in response to a child's behavior.

You've no doubt heard the saying "Spare the rod and spoil the child." This adage, gleaned from a seventeenth-century poem by Samuel Butler, is likely based on Proverbs 13:24: "Those who spare the rod of discipline hate their children. Those who love their children care enough to discipline them." So the Bible clearly teaches that discipline is necessary; in fact, it's an expression of love. How that discipline is administered has, unfortunately, become a point of division in our culture. I have no intention of embroiling myself in the controversy over spanking and other forms of discipline, but I think it's important to establish certain principles that will help clarify the role of discipline in the training of children.

Discipline is all about bringing, or allowing, appropriate consequences in response to a child's behavior.

First of all, discipline must always be seen as in the child's best interest. In that regard, it must be seen as a corrective rather than as punishment. That said, I believe discipline, in order to be effective, must bring some level of discomfort to the child when the rules have been broken or when the child has moved beyond safe boundaries. If you violate the commands of God and rebel against the security of the boundaries He has set, you are going to experience discomfort— or pain, in many cases—and sometimes the consequences are dreadful. So it's much better to learn discipline and self-control early in life through the administration of correction, rather than learn everything the hard way later on.

That's why discipline must be rooted in love for the child and why discipline—rightly applied—is always in the child's best interest. There's no question that living outside the boundaries in life is not only problematic for the person doing it, but it also affects everyone around that person, often including innocent bystanders such as a spouse, children, or friends. So to say that the consequences of willful rebellion or sin bring pain is not an exaggeration. It's simply a fact.

Therefore, when you are correcting a child, I believe there must be discomfort and often—like it or not—pain. Obviously this can be taken too far, as in cases of child abuse inflicted by out-of-control parents. We must understand that correction is never meaningful or positive if parents discipline when they are angry or out of control. Discipline must always be applied with sensitivity and with the safety and security of the child in mind, because the very purpose of discipline is to protect children and help them avoid the painful consequences of inappropriate acts of rebellion in later life.

How that discomfort is measured is seriously discussed today, and any form of physical punishment, such as spanking or using a switch, is often challenged. I disagree with those challenges except when it involves a parent who has a serious anger problem and is out of control. What Betty and I discovered in disciplining our three children was that the consistent application of appropriate discipline when our kids were young resulted in a steadily decreasing need for physical punishment as they grew up.

When we looked at the issue prayerfully, we decided that using a lightweight "switch," such as a light wooden spoon that would cause only a bit of stinging, was the most appropriate means of discipline when our children were young. The point of using the switch rather than our hand was to associate the pain with their actions rather than with our actions in correcting them. We were never cruel. Discipline was never a beating. We would say, "This is wrong. Don't do it."

As our children grew older, we corrected and disciplined them by taking away privileges. They experienced the pain or discomfort of not getting to do something they wanted to do. This form of discipline encompassed time-outs, grounding, sending a child to his or her room, or the loss of a specific privilege. Today with our grandchildren that might mean no cell phone access for a period of time, no television, computer games, use of the car, or something else the child values. The specifics vary, but the point is that the child must experience discomfort, and the discomfort must be associated with the act of disobedience or rebellion.

By the time our children reached their double digits in age, they needed little more than a word of correction. We didn't spend time screaming or yelling at them. We just told them the reality: if you go against the rules and rebel, you will suffer uncomfortable consequences. As far as spanking was concerned, the need for it diminished when our kids were relatively young.

To me, discipline fits hand in glove with the training process. If we only instruct our children and fail to link that instruction with experience, which includes consequences, then we haven't done a proper job of training. It is clearly within a child's best interest to learn to respect boundaries and to live within those guidelines. Discipline is a necessary and vital part of the learning process. Just as the principles in God's Word, His commands and His truths, are given for our benefit—not to limit our joy in life, but to increase and enhance it—so is the process of discipline intended to bring positive results in the lives of our children. Because the consequences of sin, rebellion, and evil bring about such painful consequences in life, we do our kids a disservice if we fail to train them properly within the home.

Perhaps the most important point to make about discipline within the context of this book is that husbands and wives must agree on setting boundaries and guidelines for their children. And they must help each other maintain a consistent and appropriate level of discipline. When a husband and wife balance out each other on the subject of discipline—which is the opposite of canceling out each other—the result will likely be a reasonable and appropriate level of discipline within the home. As with most things in marriage, this ultimately comes down to communication, trust, and concern.

ADMITTING OUR MISTAKES

One of the great lessons Betty and I learned when training our children was to accept that, as parents, we were going to make mistakes. It's inevitable. And just as we will face challenges in marriage, which come from our baggage and our sinful nature, we will face similar challenges as parents. We are going to mess up;

we will in some ways fail our kids. We may even unintentionally wound their spirit without knowing it. We can act out of our emotions and take things out on our kids that they don't deserve. They can frustrate us to the point where we lose our temper and snap at them.

Does any of this sound familiar? I'm not saying it is ever okay to lose control with your kids, nor am I offering any excuses for that type of behavior. All I'm saying is that, as parents, occasionally we are going to fail or disappoint our children. What do we do when this happens? How should we, as parents and as Christians who love God, handle our shortcomings? If we admit our failures, won't it defeat our purpose?

On the contrary, if there's one core truth of parenting that I've held on to throughout my years as a father and grandfather, it's this: my kids never knew me to be as right as when I admitted I was wrong. And I was wrong many times.

> *My kids never knew me to be as right as when I admitted I was wrong.*

On more than one occasion, I had to sit down with one or all of my children and say, "I'm sorry. I missed it. I didn't handle this situation correctly. I didn't consider your feelings." I've had to admit any number of mistakes, and I've done it willingly. For example, I coached my son's flag football team and the first couple of years of tackle football, and I sometimes had to correct myself in my approach to the boys. Anyone who has ever heard me speak to a church congregation or crusade knows I can be very forceful. I inspired the best in the boys on the team, and many parents reported that playing football for me was life changing for their children. But occasionally I took it too far.

After one very close game, when Randy was about ten, he and I were alone at the kitchen table after the game. I looked him in the eye and said, "Son, I was pretty hard on the boys after the game today. I had to get pretty tough and in their face. Do you think some of them might have misunderstood and even wondered if I really cared about them?"

Randy responded very softly but with a sense of confidence, "Dad, I think some of them might have misunderstood, and they might have been hurt."

"Son, I'm sorry," I said, "and I'm going to acknowledge at our next practice that I was too hard on them and ask them to forgive me." I did that, and it made an impact on all the boys, including Randy.

I also know that when our children were young, I shouted at them far too often. I could easily excuse myself by thinking, *Well, I'm always preaching to big crowds, and I've got a big voice.* But I knew that wasn't the real issue. As our children grew up, I learned to tone down, because I recognized that if you shout at your wife and children, you will raise a bunch of shouters and screamers. That's not what I wanted to do.

Taking responsibility for mistakes is one of the best things you can teach your children, and it starts with you. Your children are watching you and learning from you, whether you want them to or not. Take the responsibility to train them up, and you'll see what Betty and I see when we look at our own kids: adults who are in love with God, in love with their spouses, and in love with their own children. We are now witnessing our eleven grandchildren growing in very real and personal relationships with God. What a wonderful legacy.

ENCOURAGING ONE ANOTHER TO GROW

✦ BETTY

I think one of the reasons we are seeing such a fruitful legacy in our family is that we deliberately set out to encourage one another. This practice probably meant as much to our family as anything we ever tried in the form of a Bible study or a special devotional time.

We would gather in the family room with everyone having a little spiral notepad on which they had written something positive about each family member. Before we would meet, James would tell the children, "I want you to write down several things that you admire or really like in your brother and sister" (or "in your sisters," for Randy). Next we would have them write down things in their own lives that they thought needed to change. Then we shared our lists—both the things we liked about the others and the things in ourselves that needed to change—and we prayed for one another.

> *Some of the greatest moves of God's Spirit came in our get-togethers in the family room.*

This little exercise really helped us bond as a family. These times of sharing often were tearful, moving moments, and we all appreciated what the others said about us. And we cared about what everyone shared as personal weaknesses. We ultimately reached a point where we were close enough and had enough confidence in one another that we could identify areas in one another that needed improvement.

And, yes, James and I had the children write about us as well. We asked, "What do you see in us that you'd like to be changed?" Their feedback was a valuable means of understanding how our parenting was perceived and received.

James has noted that those times together as a family, sharing our hearts with one another, were more powerful than any church revival meeting we have ever attended. Some of the greatest moves of God's Spirit that our family witnessed came in our get-togethers in the family room. I believe that the key was the unity and the common spirit we cultivated by being open, honest, and caring about one another as we shared and prayed together.

> So commit yourselves wholeheartedly to these words of mine. Tie them to your hands and wear them on your forehead as reminders. Teach them to your children. Talk about them when you are at home and when you are on the road, when you are going to bed and when you are getting up. Write them on the doorposts of your house and on your gates. (Deuteronomy 11:18–20)

Take every opportunity to pass on to your children what you've been given by God.

FOR REFLECTION AND DISCUSSION

Why should parenting be a 100 percent team effort by mom and dad?

What areas of your parenting could use more tell *and* show—that is, both good instruction and modeling?

Why is discipline such a key part of training your child in the way he or she should go?

14

Sex

Satisfy and bless one another.

JAMES

*I*n church circles, one topic almost always causes people to squirm, either because they're embarrassed to talk about it or because they feel convicted about their own practices. Of course, we're about to discuss sex.

In our society, sex is often called "making love," but by this point in the book, it should be obvious that there's so much more to making love than simply having sex. That's not to downplay the importance of sex in a marriage; sex is an essential part of marital intimacy, but it is only a part. Sex should neither be overemphasized nor neglected.

Rightly understood, sex is one of the greatest gifts God ever gave to a man and a woman. It is a natural, exciting, and beautiful act that, when practiced in the context of a marriage based on lifelong commitment, mutual trust, and mutual concern, serves to promote complete oneness (see Genesis 2:24).

What do I mean by *oneness*? I'm talking about the oneness that Jesus prayed for in John 17. After the Last Supper, right before Jesus left the Upper Room to go to the Garden of Gethsemane, He prayed that His disciples might be one, just as Jesus and His Father are one (see John 17:11, NIV). Although in this context Jesus is praying for unity within the body of Christ, when He asks the Father for oneness, He evokes God's original design for humanity that goes all the way back to the Garden of Eden.

Think for a moment about how man and woman were created. Both were made in the image of God, and both bear attributes of God's character and personality. Yet the woman was created out of the man, and thus both sexes individually reflect certain aspects of God's character apart from the other. With that in mind, it seems clear that in the joining of a man and a woman in marriage, we see a restoration of the original unity of mankind as made in the image of God. We also see a reflection of the unity

There's so much more to making love than simply having sex.

and oneness that characterize the Trinity. That's why marriage can never be anything other than the union of one man and one woman. It's part of the very fabric of our humanity.

Sex is a physical representation of the leave-and-cleave commitment that you and your spouse made to each other as husband and wife. It is a holy act of unity. However, our great enemy, Satan, seeks to take the sacred and make it profane. He seeks to damage the great gifts we have received from God by twisting them around to make them inappropriately attractive and dirty. And he's done a great job with sex. Our culture has immersed itself in lust at an alarming rate and has become very adept at making sex seem like a casual, harmless practice that is healthy for anyone, anywhere, anytime.

This perception couldn't be further from the truth. In 1 Corinthians 6:15–20, the apostle Paul sets the record straight and provides an eloquent counterpoint to our society's debased view of sex:

> Don't you realize that your bodies are actually parts of Christ? Should a
> man take his body, which is part of Christ, and join it to a prostitute?

Never! And don't you realize that if a man joins himself to a prostitute, he becomes one body with her? For the Scriptures say, "The two are united into one." But the person who is joined to the Lord is one spirit with him.

Run from sexual sin! No other sin so clearly affects the body as this one does. For sexual immorality is a sin against your own body. Don't you realize that your body is the temple of the Holy Spirit, who lives in you and was given to you by God? You do not belong to yourself, for God bought you with a high price. So you must honor God with your body.

If the joining of a man and a woman in marriage illustrates the complete nature of God—encompassing both male and female, as well as representing the oneness and unity of God in His triune nature—is it any wonder that Satan focuses his attack on marriage in general and on individual marriages in particular?

ONENESS IS POSSIBLE

When Jesus prayed that we would be one as He and the Father are one, it meant that unity and oneness are possible. Would God deny His Son's request? Jesus said that in oneness we are perfected in unity (see John 17:23). So unity and one-ness are hallmarks of a marriage dedicated to God. But what does that mean in practical terms, and what does that have to do with sex?

When, through the power of the Holy Spirit and our faith in Jesus Christ, we become one with God, as Jesus prayed we would, the following characteristics (among others) will be evident in our lives:

- We will desire to please Him.
- We will desire to do His will.
- We will desire to learn.
- We will desire to grow.
- We will desire to be corrected and correctable.

- We will desire to be teachable.
- We will desire to be meek (which means our strength will be yielded to God).

All these same principles apply to the sexual union in a marriage relationship:

- We will desire to please each other.
- We will desire to submit ourselves to each other, body and soul.
- We will desire to learn with and from each other.
- We will desire to grow together in oneness of heart, mind, and soul.
- We will desire to be corrected and correctable so we're not taking advantage of each other.
- We will desire to be teachable.
- We will desire to yield our strength to each other.

We want to have all these things in our sexual relationship, but in order for that to happen, we must first submit ourselves to God and desire oneness with Him. If we seek complete harmony with the heart of God, then we can have oneness in marriage as far as sex is concerned and, in fact, in every area of our life.

Do you see how the perspective of pursuing oneness takes our understanding of sex—as well as our valuing of sex—beyond the emphasis on frequency, positions, and methods that captivates popular culture?

SEX AS A SAFE PLACE

✦ BETTY

God wants us to enjoy His gift of sex in the way He intended. He gave husbands and wives the joy and privilege of pursuing a meaningful physical relationship in order to deepen their intimacy and strengthen their marriage. Through sex, spouses can learn how to share certain feelings and desires with each other that couldn't—and shouldn't—be discussed with anyone else. Through sex, spouses can learn how to open themselves up to each other, allowing access into the deepest part of their heart and soul. Sex is a physical expression of their spiritual commitment to each other and of the type of meaningful, open, and honest communication they desire. It is a beautiful experience, beyond anyone's ability to adequately describe—much like the beauty found in the experience of true love.

James and I discussed earlier how the marriage relationship needs to be a safe place in which we trust each other enough to bare our heart as well as our body. The foundation for this safe place is established in the bedroom. When as husbands and wives we connect intimately through sex, we unlock the door to open, honest, heart-to-heart communication.

James and I have always talked openly with each other about our feelings, concerns, and desires, not just about sex, but about life in general. Part of the reason we are able to discuss our innermost thoughts on a broad range of topics is because we've learned how to be intimate through sex. We came to a point where we knew we could trust each other; we didn't have to worry that we were going to upset the other person by expressing our deep-seated thoughts, feelings, or desires. By creating a safe haven in the bedroom, we reinforced the safety of our overall relationship. Through the gift of intimacy, I was able to let James know he was safe with me, and he let me know I was safe with him. It reinforced the feeling that our love was real and that it would endure no matter what. This safety and security has translated into a lifetime of open and honest communication in all areas of life.

But as wonderful a gift as sex is, it creates a potential pitfall for many marriages. Because of the intimate nature of sex, and the strong desire most people have for it, it can quickly become an unhealthy pursuit. Husbands can easily indulge in lustful thinking and corrupt the marriage bed. Wives can withhold sex in an attempt

> *By creating a safe haven in the bedroom, we reinforced the safety of our overall relationship.*

to exert power over their husbands and manipulate them. That's why it's not helpful to talk about sex outside the full context of the marriage relationship.

As much as our society wants us to believe that sex is simply a fun way to experience the thrill of ecstasy, the truth is that ecstasy apart from commitment, trust, and mutual care and concern is a dead-end street. In fact, it's quite damaging. Sex is designed to be an expression of commitment and genuine intimacy that only a husband and wife can share. In any other context, it eventually and inevitably degrades our humanity. It assassinates us even as it fascinates us. But within the safe haven of a loving, committed marriage, sex becomes an expression of the fullness of our humanity.

FREEDOM IN THE BEDROOM

✦ JAMES

The bedroom must be a safe place where a couple can feel free to satisfy and bless each other through sexual expression, yielding themselves completely to each other. The Scriptures teach, "The wife does not have authority over her own body, but the husband does; and likewise also the husband does not have authority over his own body, but the wife does" (1 Corinthians 7:4, NASB). I believe this means that, as a couple, you are free to express your desires and explore sensual pleasures for the pure joy you can experience in this God-given relationship, provided both you and your spouse are comfortable with those particular expressions. This is one of the many reasons that God designed sex to be experienced within the bonds of marriage. It is directly linked to the commitment and communication your marriage needs in order to thrive.

I believe you must be able to be honest with each other about your interests and your desires—even your curiosity. As a husband, I can tell you that I'm 100 percent committed to anything that would excite my wife or give her joy or pleasure in any area of her life, including sexually. At the same time, I'm 100 percent respectful of what she wants, desires, and needs. Because our marriage is based on mutual commitment, trust, and concern, I want only what is in Betty's best interests.

I also want to feel free to share with Betty my own desires and interests, including sexually, and to be able to talk to her. And I can. If your marriage is based on commitment, trust, communication, and concern for each other, you're not going to do something or demand something of your spouse that is disrespectful or shaming. And if you have good communication in your relationship, then whatever you work out between the two of you should be fine. And it's really nobody else's business.

What Betty and I have discovered in our journey—and this has been validated by talking to counselors and other couples—is that husbands and wives must agree about what is meaningful to them. That's true in all aspects of a marriage relationship but particularly when it comes to sex. The bedroom is a very personal and private place between a husband and a wife; it's a sacred place in which they can pursue and explore true intimacy. When you are experiencing this most intimate of times, your focus should be entirely on the other person as you lose yourselves in each other. Intimacy can be understood as "into me see" as couples open up and reveal their hearts, their desires, and their passions.

In order for sex to be all that it can be, both spouses must feel free to express their desire to give pleasure to the other person. It's not that they don't care about their own satisfaction, but they find greater fulfillment in knowing they have given pleasure to the other person. We should be motivated when our spouse is excited about having a pleasurable experience. I believe, as husbands, we should always be interested in taking the time to give our wife pleasure.

Intimacy can be understood as "into me see" as couples open up and reveal their hearts, their desires, and their passions.

If you're genuinely going to be one flesh in your marriage in the way God intends, you're also going to become one in spirit, soul, and heart. Husbands, that means you will love your wife as Christ loved the church, giving yourself up for her (see Ephesians 5:25). Wives, that means you will submit yourself to your husband as unto the Lord (see Ephesians 5:22).

These verses in Ephesians have been the subject of much discussion and controversy in the church and certainly in our society. But to my way of thinking, they're pretty straightforward. Husbands, if you will focus your attention on loving your wife as Christ loved the church—and read the Gospels to discover what Jesus did in that regard—the submission part will take care of itself. It's a matter of leadership and commitment. Wives, I think you'll agree that if your husband loves you sacrificially, godly submission to him won't be an issue. If both spouses work together to honor God and each other, these so-called controversial scriptural commandments will not become divisive.

THE SECRET

Men, you've no doubt heard the saying "Sex begins in the kitchen," which Dr. Kevin Leman used as the focus of one of his books. What that means, I think, is that what happens outside the bedroom is just as important as what happens inside the bedroom. As we've established in this chapter, a meaningful and fulfilling sexual relationship in marriage begins with a meaningful and fulfilling relationship. Period. It's impossible to overestimate the importance of commitment, trust, communication, and concern in creating the environment in which a satisfying sexual relationship can develop.

If there's a secret formula for a mutually satisfying sexual relationship in marriage, here's what I believe it is: cultivating your desire to be together. Think back to what initially attracted you to your mate. Was it not simply a desire to be together? Most couples in the early stages of their relationship will move heaven and earth to find time to be together. Staying up late, getting up early, driving across town or across the country—whatever it took, they were willing.

Remember those days?

What happened?

What Betty and I have discovered in our marriage and have observed in other marriages that have stood the test of time is that the simple desire to be together is an important cornerstone in a lasting, exciting marriage. We really want to be with each other. The couples who thrive are the ones who enjoy being together, and they make it a priority to spend time together. Their lives are not boring but an ongoing adventure.

If simply being together remains a priority in your marriage, such closeness will spill over into the bedroom. But time together doesn't just happen. It has to be cultivated, nurtured, protected. That means finding an opportunity to be away from the children for a while. It means finding a way to set aside other distractions and to overcome busyness and fatigue.

For many couples, especially those with small children, this is a major issue. Couples who are busy with children, long hours on the job, or work-related travel may benefit by scheduling sex on their calendars. Making an appointment may seem less spontaneous and fun, but it can help both spouses to think about sex during the day and look forward to a special evening together. Simply put, if the relationship itself is important, then what happens within the relationship will be a reflection of that.

The good news is that couples who have a healthy sex life will reap numerous physical benefits as well. God knew what He was doing when He gave us this precious gift! Studies have shown that sex not only boosts immunity but also relieves stress and improves cardiovascular health. It can reduce pain and the risk for prostate cancer. Sex also increases levels of oxytocin, the hormone known for helping couples to bond and build trust. If you want to enjoy emotional intimacy in your marriage, engaging in regular physical intimacy is imperative. The two cannot be separated.[1]

When husbands and wives define their top sexual needs, near the top of

> *If you want to enjoy emotional intimacy in your marriage, engaging in regular physical intimacy is imperative.*

the list for both men and women is the need to feel valued, affirmed, and desired. Men and women may express that desire in different ways, but the basic motivation is the same. A man wants to believe that his wife enjoys their relationship, and a woman wants to know that her husband really enjoys being with her all the time, not just in the bedroom. In fact, if your definition of being together doesn't extend beyond the bedroom, you will undercut the process of true intimacy and make the very thing you desire less attainable.

If wanting to be together and to be intimate was your great desire initially, then I think it should be maintained. If you will make your relationship a priority, you will reap the rewards of true intimacy. Betty and I have been married forty-seven years, and just being together is still an exciting priority for both of us.

AVOIDING THE DANGER ZONE

We are constantly bombarded with the world's ideas about sex and sexuality. All we have to do is open our eyes. Images that are designed to stir up lust are everywhere: billboards, television, movies, magazines, tabloids, the Internet. They're inescapable. In general, men have a visual emphasis on taking in and responding to the world, and they don't need much enticement to dip into lustful ways of thinking or addictive practices. If we don't have a place where we can openly discuss these attractive distractions, we can become entrapped.

What do we do with feelings of lust or thoughts of infidelity? With the allure of the sexually explicit material readily available today, is it even possible to live a sexually pure life? Satan and the world around us would certainly like us to believe it isn't. The Bible, however, disagrees and says that those who are committed to God through His Son, Jesus Christ, have power over sin (see Romans 5:17; 1 Corinthians 15:57). We also know that the devil is a liar (see John 8:44). We know that God's power within us is greater than the power that is in the world (see 1 John 4:4). And we know that if we obey God, He will make us "the head and not the tail" (Deuteronomy 28:13).

The Gospels say that when Jesus came, as the chief cornerstone of God's plan of redemption, anyone who opposed Him would be "broken to pieces" (Matthew 21:44; Luke 20:18). If we will take refuge in Jesus, He will empower us to walk over the schemes of the Enemy as if they were dust beneath our feet. It is possible to live in purity but not if we're unaware of the dangers or if we're unwilling to submit ourselves to God.

Let's look at what Paul says about avoiding the danger zone of sexual temptation:

> If you think you are standing strong, be careful not to fall. The temptations in your life are no different from what others experience. And God is faithful. He will not allow the temptation to be more than you can stand. When you are tempted, he will show you a way out so that you can endure. (1 Corinthians 10:12–13)

Even when the Enemy is coming at you full force, lying to you, trying to isolate you, hoping you'll feel hopeless against temptation, remember there is a way out. God is faithful. If you will seek Him and submit yourself to Him, He will show you a means of escape.

But even before temptation comes, it's possible—and prudent—to establish safe boundaries around your marriage, especially in your relationships with members of the opposite sex at work, at church, or in the neighborhood.

One of our guests on *Life Today*, a professor at Dallas Theological Seminary, shared candidly about a situation earlier in her marriage when she had to establish some explicit boundaries. At the time she was serving as president of her local PTA. Although she was a Christian and had a wonderful husband, she found herself becoming attracted to the school principal. She recognized the problem and the situations that were contributing to it, and she established some boundaries to put natural distance between herself and the principal. For example, she avoided going on a trip that would have involved traveling with the principal. She didn't feel the need to resign from her post, but she took the necessary steps to prevent an emotional affair from taking root.

I have seen on more than one occasion an improper physical relationship arise between two people, not because they were seeking sex, but because they were seeking an emotional response or validation they weren't getting at home. I've even seen it in my own ministry and by observing others both in ministry and in the business community. Women who have not seen spiritual strength and a sensitive heart in their husband or father will often be attracted to these qualities when they see them in another man, including pastors or other church leaders. What starts as a casual conversation may result in a soul connection that leads to moral compromise.

In my own experience, the women who were drawn to me in my ministry were not attracted merely because of sex; they were seeking authority, sensitivity, strength, and validation, which I unknowingly provided. On the flip side, men who stumble into inappropriate relationships are often looking for validation of themselves and their strength as men. For a man, if a woman other than his wife begins to meet that need—especially if she's physically attractive and therefore triggering his visual sensors as well—and if he isn't being validated at home, he can be vulnerable to temptation.

Although men and women approach the subject differently, I think it boils down to the same thing for both: they want to feel valued, desired, and needed. Over time those things can diminish in a marriage as couples take each other for granted. And then, whether it's in the workplace, the neighborhood, at church, or even in a counseling session, if one spouse finds a person who will pay attention or listen, it can create temptation. It doesn't even have to be flirting or anything overt. It can be as simple as a smile, something that says, "I enjoy talking with or being with you. I care about you, and I understand." Whether it's something that's said or a nonverbal cue or even a sense that someone desires you, it's an incredible force. In cases like these, it's important to recognize what is happening and to take steps to shut it down before it goes too far. We need to be honest about our emotional state and take it to the Lord, to our spouse, and, more than likely, to a marriage counselor or someone who will hold us accountable.

The antidote in a marriage is to cultivate the desire to be alone together and to be intimate. Spouses have to work to make it clear to each other how important their time together is, which brings us back to the importance of communication and concern for the other person's well-being.

The fact that individuals having an affair will go to any lengths to be together should give us some insight into how to preserve our marriage. I believe that married couples should be committed to time alone together and to intimacy, as befits two people in love. Only compelling responsibilities or a commitment to pray should ever keep them apart, and then only temporarily.

There's no substitute for time together to keep a marriage strong and vibrant.

PREVENTING ATTRACTION DISTRACTION

✦ BETTY

One of the greatest gifts a woman can give her husband is the freedom to be honest about his attractions. I think it's difficult sometimes for women to understand just how visually oriented most men are. In the same way that most women are stirred by romance, nonsexual touch, and meaningful communication, most men are stirred by what they see. This affects a marriage in two important ways: one inside the marriage and the other outside.

Inside the marriage, because a man is visually stimulated, he wants to be able to see his wife. So it can become a problem if the wife always wants to turn out the lights or if she's bothered by the fact that her husband wants to see her body. Some women say, "Well, I don't like the way I look," and that may be true, but the husband still likes the way she looks. Husbands, it's important that you never make your wife feel as if she's not beautiful when she's already fighting that battle on her own. A woman needs all the help she can get in feeling good about herself. She must never feel that her husband is comparing her to other women. *Never!*

James has always told me, and made me feel, that I'm beautiful. And I have appreciated his encouragement. But that hasn't stopped me from fighting the same battle that every woman fights when she looks at herself in the mirror. I haven't always liked what I've seen, especially early in our marriage when my sense of self-worth was so low, but it's also true even now as I'm in my sixties. I believe that women are as quick to compare themselves to other women as men are—and it's always a mistake. It's tragic for a woman to compare herself to others, and it is horrible beyond description for a man to compare his wife to other women or even to make her think that he has.

One of the greatest gifts a woman can give her husband is the freedom to be honest about his attractions.

The truth of the matter is that we've been given our body and our appearance by God. Although we must be good stewards of what we've been given, we shouldn't compare ourselves to others, especially not to the images we see in magazines and other media. Even the models themselves can't measure up in their day-to-day life to those airbrushed images, and many of them openly confess that they don't like what they see in the mirror either!

There's no end to the alluring images we all must face. Entire industries are devoted to the sole purpose of catching our attention and getting a response. As everyone knows, sex sells. But that doesn't mean a man has to be a victim. You can't control what you happen to see, but you can control what you do with that visual image. If you look a second time or stare, you may be tempted to cross the line into sexual impurity. If your desire is to please God, honor your wife, and strengthen your marriage, you will learn to appreciate the beauty of all God's creation—including attractive women—without allowing it to become a distraction.

James and I were at a restaurant recently when I noticed a truly striking young woman. I tapped James's foot under the table and said, "You need to look over your right shoulder."

"Why?" he said.

"Because you wouldn't want to miss that."

James turned and looked, and when he turned back, he smiled and said, "You were right!" And then we just grinned at each other. I was able to do that because James, over the years, has continually built me up by telling me how pretty he thinks I am. Also, in our relationship we have built a foundation of respect, love, trust, and security with each other. I didn't feel threatened or less beautiful because an attractive woman walked into the restaurant. I knew I could trust my husband to notice her beauty and that would be the end of it.

Wives, I believe we do our husbands a disservice if we think—or expect—that they're not going to notice when a beautiful woman walks by. *We* notice a gorgeous figure, so why wouldn't a man? At the same time, husbands, your wife needs to be able to trust that you're not going to start thinking improper thoughts. When there is mutual respect and trust in a relationship, it should result in greater freedom and honesty—even in acknowledging outside attractions.

If we make our husband feel ashamed or that he has to act as if he didn't notice, we force him into hiding and living in pretense, which undermines the very foundation of our relationship. I believe it's much more constructive and rewarding if a wife can provide a place of safety where her husband is free to be honest and where both spouses can battle these temptations and distractions together.

ONLINE AND OFF TRACK

✦ JAMES

I must address one of the gravest threats to men in our society: online visual traps. Whether it's outright pornography or merely suggestive photos, videos, and articles, the temptations available on the Internet are almost beyond belief.

Women can be caught in these same snares, but men by far are more at risk. If King David, one of the greatest men ever to live—a man after God's own heart, according to 1 Samuel 13:14—can be distracted by a glimpse from his balcony of a woman taking a bath, what about men who have access to unlimited on-line glimpses? Every man today, at the touch of his fingers, can access images of beautiful women doing far more than bathing.

The lure of pornography is a potential problem in every marriage. That's why Paul is so adamant that we must flee from sexual impurity. It damages the body (see 1 Corinthians 6:15–20) and harms our relationships. When we give in to the temptation to look at pornography, I believe we create an appetite that's every bit as powerful as those we might provoke through gluttony, drugs, or alcohol. Sexual impurity creates unhealthy appetites and desires that should never be stirred. We need to understand—even from childhood—that we must seek to avoid sexual temptation in all its forms.

When I speak to teenagers, I bring this up because I know from my own experience how powerful and seductive pornographic images can be. When I was about twelve years old, I was riding my bike and came across a stash of pornography lying in a neighbor's yard. Let me tell you, I'm sixty-six years old, and I can *still* see some of those images in my mind's eye—that's how indelibly they're burned into my brain. Someone once described looking at pornographic images as putting a tattoo on the brain.

If pornography or other sexual immorality has you in its jaws, get help to get out.

I've talked to so many men who struggle with pornography. They say it can quickly become an eight-hundred-pound gorilla on your back. Husbands and wives and the church at large need to respond to this epidemic in our society with loving, caring, and uncompromising concern for the men and women caught in the pornography trap. Only God can truly set us free, but there's much we can do to avoid the problem or at least deal with it candidly and completely when it rears its ugly head.

I want to say this as clearly and forcefully as I can: If pornography or other sexual immorality has you in its jaws, get help to get out. And if you aren't ensnared, do everything you can to avoid the trap. If that means giving up some features or functions on your computer to put safeguards in place, then do it. If that means showing your wife everything you're looking at online, then do it. Choose freedom over bondage, honesty over deception. With God's help, you can do it, but you must exercise your own will to take the necessary steps. The payoff of purity in your life and your marriage will be well worth it.

WHEN TRUST HAS BEEN BROKEN

What do you do if you have given in to temptation, acted on improper feelings, and betrayed your spouse?

If you have encountered a sexual challenge or obstacle in your marriage, your first move is to turn to God. Jesus walked this earth for thirty-three years as a flesh-and-blood human being. He knows how you feel. The Bible tells us in 1 Corinthians 10:13, "The temptations in your life are no different from what others experience." Jesus was just as much man as He was God, so any temptation you've experienced, He did too.

One of the devil's big tricks is to flaunt sexuality all over the place, and when people give in to sexual temptation, he tries to convince them that they're the only ones dealing with that particular sin. The truth is, when it comes to sin, you and I are nothing special. We're just like everyone else. So just like everyone else, when we sin, our first step is to take our sin to Jesus and ask Him for forgiveness.

As we saw earlier, sexual sin is unique in one respect: it is "a sin against your own body" (1 Corinthians 6:18). Because you and your spouse are united as one, a sin against yourself is also a sin against your spouse. That means you need to bring your husband or wife into the loop. As difficult as it may be to confess that you've sinned sexually, your spouse needs to know.

The way in which this is done is very important. It's not just about getting something off your chest. You must consider the heart of your spouse and the hurt that will be caused by your confession. You must approach him or her with a sincere spirit of brokenness and repentance, and you have to be prepared for how he or she may respond.

Remember what I said earlier about confession, about having a sticker removed from your paw, which I occasionally have to do for our dog, Princess? Admitting to sexual sin is going to hurt, and it will most likely damage your relationship for a time. Ultimately, however, it is a necessary hurt in order to move toward reconciliation and restoration. With God's help, the hurt will heal, making you even stronger than you were before.

What if you are the one sinned against? I encourage spouses who have been wounded not to immediately throw in the towel. Instead, seek a good, Bible-believing marriage counselor to help you through this difficult time and shepherd your marriage back to the place where it needs to be. I have observed that most sexual sin in marriage comes, not from a place of sexuality, but rather from emotional hurt or pain. A pastor or counselor can help you and your spouse communicate more effectively and provide a safe, neutral place for you to work through these issues. You will need help to overcome feelings of betrayal, to learn to trust again, and to develop an attitude of forgiveness and restoration in your marriage.

REBUILD TRUST?

The process of restoring trust when it has been broken is beyond the scope of this book, but if you're in that situation, Betty and I urge you to find the help you need. Seek the Lord's strength and don't automatically write off your spouse. We know it's difficult, but if you can rely on the grace of God to cultivate forgiveness in your heart, and if you can choose to help your spouse and face this challenge together, your marriage will have a greater chance of surviving and ultimately thriving. Yes, it is possible!

Betty and I have seen many marriages that—from a human perspective—seemed beyond repair. But God put those marriages back together, and many of them are stronger than before. We have to recognize and acknowledge that many people—both men and women—come into marriage as damaged goods. Whether it's the result of abuse, neglect, dysfunction, violence, or willful disobedience, many people carry a heavy load of baggage and pain. It can take both the grace of God and an understanding mate to repair the damage. If your spouse comes to you acknowledging a problem, don't dismiss or interrupt his or her confession. If he or she trusts you and respects you enough to confess—even if what is confessed is hurtful and reveals a lack of respect and trustworthiness—there is hope for reconciliation and restoration. If you bury your spouse after a confession because you're hurt and angry, you may keep your spouse from getting the help he or she needs.

Obviously, betrayal hurts. But if you can avoid throwing stones, if you can rely on God to heal the pain and restore the relationship, you can have a marriage that rises from the ashes and thrives.

FOR REFLECTION AND DISCUSSION

What is the difference between making love and having sex?

What are some of the ways a couple can establish a safe place for sex in their marriage?

What poses the greatest threat to genuine physical intimacy in your marriage?

15

The Invisible Enemy

The destroyer of marriages never rests.

JAMES

*A*re you aware that there is a hidden, evil force attacking you, your spouse, and those you dearly love? Through subtle deception and distraction, this enemy far too often accomplishes his deadly goal. Both the Old and New Testaments reveal the reality that this battle in the spiritual realm affects everything in the physical realm. If Betty and I had not discovered the truth shared in this chapter, our relationship could have been severely damaged or destroyed many years ago.

God established the covenant of marriage for many reasons, but one of the most important is to serve as a picture of the relationship between Jesus and His people. In God's design for marriage, your relationship with your spouse represents the ultimate triumph of good over evil. And because that's true, Satan hates the institution of marriage and will do everything he can to destroy it. The full force of his fury is focused on everything sacred, especially the intimacy in our relationships.

First, the Enemy attacks our intimacy with God, trying to isolate us from our defender and the source of all our power.

Next, he attacks the intimacy between husbands and wives, trying to damage or destroy the unity that God desires for marriage—the unity that God designed as a reflection of the relationship within the Trinity.

In God's design for marriage, your relationship with your spouse represents the ultimate triumph of good over evil.

The Enemy also attacks us within the family, both the family structure in society and the family of God, the church. In Revelation, Satan is referred to as the "accuser of our brothers and sisters," and our spiritual enemy very subtly leads spouses, siblings, and fellow church members often to be seen as one another's accusers (see 12:10).

Satan doesn't waste his time on the people he already controls. In fact, he'll build them up, make them look good, and give them the kingdoms of the world. Part of the Enemy's strategy is to make people believe that they don't need God or that God can't save them.

When Satan attacks believers, he tries to tear up everything we have. The Bible describes his tactics in 1 Peter 5:8: "Stay alert! Watch out for your great enemy, the devil. He prowls around like a roaring lion, looking for someone to devour."

Satan is a predator looking for prey. He's looking for every weakness and every opportunity to rush in and devour. Is it any wonder, then, that marriages everywhere are under pressure and under attack? The devil knows that if he can drive a wedge into a marriage and create distance, friction, or discord between a husband and wife, both spouses become more vulnerable.

But here's the good news: you and your spouse don't have to be like meek little gazelles on the African savanna, awaiting your fate in the lion's jaws. You don't have to lie down and accept the devil's tricks and tactics to defeat you. And you don't have to run. In fact, running in fear is the worst thing you can do, because it only puts the devil in pursuit as he tries to bring down the vulnerable, the weak, and the wounded. When the roaring lion comes to devour us, the apostle Peter says, "Stand firm against him, and be strong in your faith" (1 Peter 5:9). And James says, "Resist the devil, and he will flee from you" (James 4:7). Did you catch that? *He* will flee from *you!*

You can walk in victory over the Enemy in your life and in your marriage. You can stand firm and be strong in your faith—but how? Both Peter and James give the same counsel:

Humble yourselves before God. Resist the devil, and he will flee from you. Come close to God, and God will come close to you. (James 4:7–8)

Humble yourselves before the Lord, and he will lift you up in honor. (James 4:10)

Humble yourselves under the mighty power of God, and at the right time he will lift you up in honor. (1 Peter 5:6)

Your marriage is under bombardment by intruders in the spiritual realm, and the only way to thwart those attacks is to humble yourself before God and stand firm in your faith.

How do you humble yourself before God? One way is to *believe* what He says, *submit* yourself to His guidance and direction, and *act* on the truth He has revealed in the Bible. The truth is, you're not alone in this battle. In fact, "Greater is He who is in you than he who is in the world" (1 John 4:4, NASB). The apostle Paul describes the mighty weapons we have available as followers of Jesus:

For though we walk in the flesh, we do not war according to the flesh. For the weapons of our warfare are not carnal but mighty in God for pulling down strongholds, casting down arguments and every high thing that exalts itself against the knowledge of God, bringing every thought into captivity to the obedience of Christ. (2 Corinthians 10:3–5, NKJV)

Be strong in the Lord and in the power of His might. Put on the whole armor of God, that you may be able to stand against the wiles of the devil. For we do not wrestle against flesh and blood, but against principalities, against powers, against the rulers of the darkness of this age, against spiritual hosts of wickedness in the heavenly places. Therefore take up the whole armor of God, that you may be able to withstand in the evil day, and having done all, to stand.

Stand therefore, having girded your waist with truth, having put on the breastplate of righteousness, and having shod your feet with the preparation of the gospel of peace; above all, taking the shield of faith with which you will be able to quench all the fiery darts of the wicked one. And take the helmet of salvation, and the sword of the Spirit, which is the word of God; praying always with all prayer and supplication in the Spirit, being watchful to this end with all perseverance and supplication for all the saints. (Ephesians 6:10–18, NKJV)

In order to resist the work of the devil in your life, you must first be humble enough to admit that you can't go it alone and that you need the supernatural power of God to lift you up, set your feet on a firm foundation, and enable you to resist the schemes of Satan. And then you must *use* the weapons that are available.

Too many Christian couples try to ignore the Enemy rather than resist him.

One reason we've included a chapter on spiritual warfare in a book about marriage is that far too many Christian couples try to ignore the Enemy rather than resist him. It's as Betty said about her upbringing: she thought if she just left the devil alone, he'd leave her alone as well.

But it doesn't work that way. Our spiritual enemy is constantly on the prowl, seeking whom he might devour. Nothing will make you and your marriage more vulnerable to the attack of this "accuser of our brothers and sisters" than acting as if he doesn't exist. Unfortunately, that's what many people seem to do. If we were to recognize the reality of spiritual warfare and take the steps described in Scripture to resist the devil, we would do a much better job of standing firm and walking in freedom. In Jesus's temptation by the devil in the wilderness, we can witness three examples of Satan's tactics and how we can overcome temptation through God's Word (see Luke 4).

THE SIFTING WORK OF SATAN

✦ BETTY

I recognize now that early in our marriage I was oppressed by tormenting spirits. (The Bible specifically mentions some of these harassing spirits by name— for example, the spirit of deception, bondage, and torment—as well as referring numerous times to demons as evil, foul, or unclean.) I just assumed there was something wrong with me, and there was, but I didn't know the true source of my problem. I didn't know anything about a "spirit of fear"[1]; I just knew I was afraid of being found out, of being judged, of not measuring up, and of letting people down. This fear manifested itself as low self-esteem, avoidance of conflict, and persistent feelings of inadequacy. Furthermore, I was trapped by a spirit of performance that made me believe I had to do everything perfectly in order to be accepted. However, Scripture clearly tells us that God did not give us a spirit of fear but of power, love, and a sound mind.[2]

Now with more than forty years of perspective and with greater understanding of the devil's schemes, I see how Satan attacked me at my points of weakness and tried to paralyze me and keep me distant from God. Taking advantage of my feelings of inadequacy, he sought to drive a wedge between James and me and undermine our marriage.

Satan so deceived me early in our marriage that I was convinced I was going to die young, and then James would get the kind of wife he deserved—someone more suitable.

What a cruel liar Satan is! But I bought into it. James did his best to encourage me and to make me feel smart and attractive, but there was an ongoing battle in my mind and in my heart. Over time I found that I relied too heavily on James for my sense of well-being and my security.

Then, at the height of his success, James began to burn out in his crusade ministry. He became discouraged, defeated, and emotionally, physically, and spiritually depleted. One of the people he turned to for help was his friend Dudley Hall, a Bible teacher who had spoken at several of our Bible conferences and had conducted follow-up seminars after the crusades. James described to him an inward impression that "felt like a claw" in his brain, and it was oppressing him and wouldn't let go. He told Dudley that he couldn't seem to control his appetites, anger, and lustful thoughts.

When Dudley began to talk about strongholds and the effect that Satan can have on the lives of Christians, I didn't know what to think. I had always assumed that when we placed our faith in Christ, we became immune to the works of the devil, even though that teaching cannot be found in the Bible.

I've since learned that becoming a Christian is like painting a bull's-eye on our back at which the Enemy takes aim. The fury of the Enemy is focused on God's purpose for our lives, beginning with our intimacy with God and extending to our marriage and family relationships. Even when we are walking closely with God, just as Jesus did in Luke 4, Satan looks for every opportunity to bring us down.

> *Becoming a Christian is like painting a bull's-eye on our back at which the Enemy takes aim.*

Think about what happened to one of Jesus's closest disciples, Simon Peter. At the Last Supper, Jesus said to him, "Simon, Simon, behold, Satan has demanded permission to sift you like wheat; but I have prayed for you, that your faith may not fail; and you, when once you have turned again, strengthen your brothers" (Luke 22:31–32, NASB). If one so close to Jesus could be sifted like wheat by Satan, why would we expect anything different? If bold, courageous Peter, the rugged fisherman who had said, "Others may leave you, but I won't,"[3] could find himself only hours later denying Jesus three times, is that not evidence enough that the devil has some influence over us?

James and I don't believe it's possible for a Christian to be possessed by an evil spirit, but without a doubt it's possible to be oppressed by evil spirits who seek out our weak points and apply pressure, accusations, and condemnation in their efforts to defeat us.

Peter's weakness might very well have been his self-sufficient confidence that he alone, of all the disciples, would remain true to Jesus. He clearly had a spirit of arrogance and pride. But in the sifting process, he became subject to a spirit of fear, denial, and deception, and his confidence, self-assurance, and personal strength melted away.

As believers we are subject to that same kind of demonic or devilish interference. When evil spirits influence us, we often behave out of character with our basic nature. Peter was not a coward, but when he tried to stand in his own strength, he acted like a coward under the attack of Satan.

That's how the Enemy works. Whenever he finds a weakness in us that might otherwise be a strength—like Peter's pride in his boldness—he rushes in and tries to take us down and drag us to the slaughter.

In James's case, the closer he came to God's deliverance, the more Satan sought to inject fear and apprehension into our hearts. When a good friend suggested that James meet with Milton Green because he knew a great deal about spiritual darkness and the effects the demonic world can have on Christians, James was uncomfortable, and I was gripped with fear, mostly of the unknown. The very mention of "spiritual darkness" or the "demonic world" made my skin crawl, and a voice inside me warned, "Don't go near this man."

As it turned out, though, God used the prayers of Milton Green in a miraculous way to set James free. I remember James waking me up in the wee hours of the morning and saying, "It's gone! It's gone!"

"What's gone?" I asked.

"Betty, something has happened in my heart and in my mind. That claw in my brain is gone. I can think! My mind is clear!"

WHEN GOD DELIVERS

✦ JAMES

Even though Betty had prayed for my deliverance and a return to the peace I had known early in our marriage, she didn't like it when it finally came. She had seen me beaten down, worn out, and dragged through the mud to the point that I didn't even want to wake up in the morning. But when the Lord heard my cry, lifted me out of the terrible pit, and put my feet on a solid rock, the dramatic change was too much for Betty. It overwhelmed and scared her.

Betty had been praying for me to get fixed, but she didn't realize she needed to get fixed too. She wanted me to get help, but when she saw the total joy of the Lord and the peace of God in my life, she didn't know quite what to make of it. I was suddenly controlled by the spirit of love, joy, peace, patience, and self-control. I was also free from religious tradition and the fear of what others thought or said about me. A river of life was flowing freely from deep within my heart.

I remember our daughter Rhonda, who was a teenager at the time, staring at me with tears of joy in her eyes one day and saying, "Daddy, you're so different." And I was! When that yoke of oppression was lifted off me, the change was so remarkable that people would say they almost didn't recognize me. One of my staff members said, "You were like a wounded bear when we had meetings with you. Now you're just like a big old bowl of love!"

As often happens when a radical change occurs in one partner within a marriage, the spouse who has not experienced the change tries to force the other person back into old, familiar patterns. But I wasn't going back for anything. When Betty tried to pick fights with me, I lovingly encouraged her to make her feelings known. It almost felt as if she was testing me, trying to see if the changes were real. And they were. What we didn't realize at the time was that my deliverance fed directly into Betty's feelings of inadequacy. When the Enemy lost his hold on me, he renewed his attack on Betty's self-image.

Satan, the fierce enemy of true love and life, hates it when couples communicate effectively. He doesn't like it when we're able to open up and release what's destroying us inside, because keeping us closed down and hidden is one of his ploys. When we married, Betty had unwittingly bought into that ploy.

She always thought it was remarkable that I felt so strongly about having open communication and airing things out, because I hadn't come from a background that encouraged such an approach. But I was determined that we were going to communicate openly, and it led to some rocky times, because that went against Betty's natural inclinations. I kept reaching out to her in love, because I knew help was available. Even though Betty would get angry with me and want to go off and pout and lick her wounds, I could see that her tendency to hide and avoid conflict was poisoning our relationship. What she needed was to be freed of all the junk she had been storing inside for years.

It was during this time that Betty asked if God was showing me anything about her, and I tenderly told her that I sensed she had an unteachable spirit. Of course, she didn't want to hear that, but it proved to be the catalyst that God used to set her free.

FINDING FREEDOM FROM FEAR

✦ BETTY

When James told me I had an unteachable spirit, I was so angry all I could do was storm out of the room and slam our bedroom door. I believe God was bringing these things to the surface so they could be dealt with, but Satan was attacking those very same points to drive me back into hiding and to keep me from receiving the healing and freedom I needed.

Until this time I had been mostly an observer of what God was doing in James's life, and I was thrilled. At the same time, I began to feel fearful and inadequate again. Even though I was happy that James was getting help, the realization that God wanted to make changes also in my life frightened me. I knew I needed to change, but I didn't know how God wanted to do it, and I was afraid of the unknown. Because I had no confidence in myself, I couldn't imagine what God might do with me or how He would use me.

I want life to be predictable. I like things the way they are, and I don't want anything unexpected to happen. Well, that's too bad for me, because that's not the way God works.

As God continued to refine James's character, I saw how real and permanent the changes were. As a result, the old fears deep in my soul, fears that had never been dealt with, again manifested themselves through insecurity, low self-esteem, and a lack of self-confidence.

The spiritual weight of all this began to affect me physically. I can remember days on end when I could hardly complete my housework before collapsing on the couch with a pounding headache. Rhonda would come home from school and find me lying on the sofa, completely drained of energy. Finally she asked, "Mom, why do you always have to be lying on the sofa?"

I had no explanation except that my head hurt and I felt tormented. It hurt me that my children too often saw me in that light. In retrospect I can see that God, in His mercy, was allowing the situation to reach a boiling point so I would cry out to Him for help. I believe it was God's perfect timing that led me to ask James if God was showing him anything about me. But I certainly wasn't ready for the answer.

I think the unteachable spirit James had seen in me was a defense mechanism, a symptom of a deeply rooted fear that had been in my heart for years. I was afraid that if people saw the real me, they would see an incapable person who would never be successful at anything.

The Enemy had convinced me that I wasn't very smart and that I had no real value. So if someone tried to help me deal with a weakness or showed me something I needed to change, I took it as a put-down and as further confirmation of my inadequacy.

When I stormed off to the bedroom, James stayed cool and patient. He knew God was working in my heart, so he just gathered the kids and took them out of the house to give me time to meet with God. The atmosphere in the bedroom was electric, as if I were seeing firsthand the warfare going on in my heart between the Enemy and God. As I paced angrily from one side of the room to the other, I sensed a cold, eerie presence surrounding me. In my mind's eye I saw evil, impish figures laughing and making fun of me, and I heard them hurling mocking accusations: "You can't escape. We have you now. There's no way out." I believe it was a manifestation of the spirits that had been tormenting me, and I felt paralyzed with fear.

Finally, in desperation, I fell to my knees beside the bed and cried out to God for help. Please, God, help me. I do have an unteachable spirit. Please forgive me. If You'll make these awful things go away, I'll do whatever You say.

I was crying out for freedom.

I don't recall any unusual feeling or emotions, but when I opened my eyes, the evil images were gone. My headache was gone too, and I felt like a completely different person. When I looked at myself in the mirror, for the first time in a long, long time, I was looking at a woman who was perfectly at peace.

Most of the time when God does something profound in our life, no words are adequate to describe it. It is so supernatural we can't explain it, but we know in our heart that something wonderful has taken place.

One thing I learned from this encounter with God is that He brings conviction but not condemnation. Yes, we have to repent of the mistakes we've made and the things we've done wrong, but through that conviction, God brings light, understanding, and correction. On the other hand, Satan brings condemnation and darkness. It's as if he has his foot on our neck and won't let up. I had to realize that when I was heavy-laden, with a battle going on inside me,

God was the One who convicted me, bringing me to repentance and forgiveness. The Enemy can only condemn and attempt to destroy us. God is light; Satan is darkness.

THE ANTIDOTE FOR DENIAL

✦ JAMES

Despite what I believe is the clear teaching of Scripture, many in the church still deny the reality of spiritual warfare and the influence of unclean spirits. I've heard people say, "Isn't blaming our problems on the devil just a way of shirking our own responsibility?" and "Why pay any more attention to the devil than you have to?" and "Aren't we promised victory over Satan through Christ?"

If you're one who disbelieves or denies the active work of a real and tangible enemy, let me ask you a few questions:

- Why do so many people act the way they act and live defeated lives?
- Why do people not have the courage to stand up for God or to witness to others?
- Why do people lack the discernment to know the kind of people they're following?
- Why do so many Christians seem unable to walk in the Spirit?
- Why are so many Christians defeated, addicted, and compulsive in their behavior and so hateful, critical, and divisive with their words?
- Why are couples out of harmony if there's not a spirit of disharmony?
- Why are some people compulsive eaters and gossipers?
- Why are so many married people constantly accusing, attacking, or ignoring their spouse?

- What influence is responsible for all of this in the lives of
  people?

Some thoughts originate with an invisible spiritual force. Our invisible enemy, the great deceiver and chief distracter, makes suggestions to our mind that often lodge and become, as Paul said, "fiery darts" or "flaming missiles."[4] If those fiery darts are something like bitterness, unforgiveness, lust, or compulsive behavior, they can literally become like a fire in our mind.

The apostle Paul tells us to use the shield of faith to quench those fiery darts and to "put on all of God's armor so that [we] will be able to stand firm against all strategies of the devil" (Ephesians 6:11). Why would he tell us to put on the armor and stand firm if there isn't an enemy?

Why would he tell us that "we are not fighting against flesh-and-blood enemies, but against evil rulers and authorities of the unseen world, against mighty powers in this dark world, and against evil spirits in the heavenly places" (Ephesians 6:12) if such forces don't exist or have no affect on us?

Why would Jesus say He's sending us out "as sheep among wolves" (Matthew 10:16) if there are no wolves?

Why did Jesus teach us to pray, "Rescue us from the evil one" (Matthew 6:13) if the evil one can't bother us? If we've already been delivered from evil and the Enemy is no longer a problem, why would Jesus teach His disciples to pray in such a way?

The fact is we have a spiritual enemy in the invisible realm who is attacking all our relationships, and he has set us on our heels in many ways. I think he keeps the house divided. This invisible enemy likes it when we argue about nonessentials, and he has convinced people to forsake the essentials. No doubt he has lured us away from sound doctrine, as Paul warned Timothy would happen, and now people "will follow their own desires and will look for teachers who will tell them whatever their itching ears want to hear" (2 Timothy 4:3).

Paul said we should not be ignorant of Satan's schemes (see 2 Corinthians 2:11), but we are unaware of them if we deny the reality of spiritual warfare. The antidote for denial is to study the Word of God to see what it reveals about the work of the Enemy, and then ask God to thwart the Enemy's plans and set us free.

When Betty and I married, we had no idea about the sinister forces that were warring against us. We just knew we needed God's help to get through our conflicts and tests. There wasn't anything wrong with that, but we needed a greater source of power to influence us in a positive direction rather than a negative one. We didn't know until later in our marriage the intensity of the spiritual warfare we would encounter. We wish we had learned earlier about these forces that were trying to tear our marriage apart.

FURNISHING THE SWEPT-OUT ROOMS

✦ BETTY

When James and I found deliverance from the strongholds in our lives, we still had to learn the importance of standing together against Satan's schemes, because when God removed those strongholds, there was an empty place that had to be filled with something. The Bible says, "When an evil spirit leaves a person, it goes into the desert, seeking rest but finding none. Then it says, 'I will return to the person I came from.' So it returns and finds its former home empty, swept, and in order. Then the spirit finds seven other spirits more evil than itself, and they all enter the person and live there. And so that person is worse off than before" (Matthew 12:43–45).

When God released me from the spirit of fear that had governed my life for so long, I had to fill that empty room to keep the tormentors from coming back. I had to learn how to relate to people apart from fear, and it didn't just naturally happen. God gave me supernatural help, filling my life—His temple—with love, peace, and joy, along with a sound mind in place of that overwhelming fear. I now had a sense of freedom, knowing that God had removed the spirit of fear, but I couldn't say, "Okay, I'm fixed. It's all over. I don't have to deal with that anymore." I still had to allow God to bring healing to my heart, to teach me how to resist fear, and to make me strong enough to stand against the Enemy's attacks. I also needed my husband to help me do that. Whenever I failed, I needed James to be right there to say, "Okay, we're going to stand against this together," and not to say, "Oh, I thought you had been delivered from that. Why is that coming up again?"

As with Jesus during His temptation by Satan, the Enemy looks for every opportune moment to attack us. James and I are determined to fill the house that God cleansed with the truth of His Word and to daily build up and renew our hearts and minds.

One important change that came about as a result of my deliverance was that I learned to depend on God rather than James for my sense of worth and security. Because James was my husband and because of the evident work of the Spirit in his life, I had placed James on a pedestal. I expected him to come through for me whenever I had a need, but God let me know that He, not my husband, was to be my first love and my deliverer.

When I released James from my unreasonable expectations, it removed a great pressure and burden from him to be the one who gave me joy, peace, and understanding. When I allowed Jesus to be the rightful head of our home, James was freed to take his place as my companion and friend.

I also learned that, in our daily walk as Christians, we have to be on guard. The Enemy is always on the lookout for an opportunity to attack again. It's important to understand that in this lifetime we never will escape spiritual warfare. Resisting the Enemy is a lifelong commitment, because Satan doesn't retire when we put on the armor of God.

In this lifetime we never will escape spiritual warfare.

Likewise, we can't just snap our fingers and have a whole, complete, heavenly marriage. It's a daily walk, and we must have the determination to say, "God, this marriage is worth fighting for. I want this relationship, and I'm going to submit myself to You and let You mold me and shape me to be the kind of mate I need to be so this marriage can be what You want it to be."

✦ JAMES

When we experience God's power in deliverance and freedom, we must yield our lives to the fullness of His Spirit. The Holy Spirit—whom Jesus sent as "another Helper" who will "be with you forever" (John 14:16, NASB)—will fill every yielded life with His power and fruit, and the effect will be evident. Just as the power of darkness and deception manifests its damaging characteristics, the Holy Spirit produces love, joy, peace, patience, and all the characteristics of God's nature.

As Betty and I yielded to this awesome power, we were both amazed that such love and peace actually flowed freely through us. We can train ourselves to control certain actions, but we cannot preprogram our reactions when the unexpected happens. That's when what is inside is revealed. We began to live as if we were carried by this river of life now flowing freely through each of us. Grace is truly amazing.

This experience of freedom and abounding fullness happened almost twenty years ago, just past the halfway point in our marriage. Without this supernatural encounter and its liberating truth, the joy in our relationship—and perhaps our marriage itself—would have been destroyed.

Betty and I encourage and challenge you to seek help, get free, and live your life filled with His Holy Spirit.

 FOR REFLECTION AND DISCUSSION

What evidence have you seen in your marriage or the marriage of others that reveals the activity of an invisible, evil force?

Why would Satan be so intent on messing up or breaking up a marriage?

In what ways can you allow the Holy Spirit to have a greater role in your marriage?

16

The Power of Encouragement

Lighten the other's load.

JAMES

We hope you have seen, by reading this book, that an abundant, thriving marriage is within your reach if you are willing to submit yourselves to God and to each other and to do what it takes to work toward this goal. A marriage that lasts a lifetime doesn't just happen. It takes effort, sacrifice, and more than a little patience. But by the grace of God, you can do it. A great verse to put at the center of your relationship is 1 Thessalonians 5:11: "Encourage each other and build each other up, just as you are already doing."

Husbands, one of the greatest gifts you can give your wife is affirmation and encouragement, and it doesn't cost a dime. With all my heart, my desire is to be Betty's greatest encourager. I am committed to lifting her up, not putting her down. I want to give her a shoulder to lean on and to provide her a sense of security in our relationship.

Our ultimate security, of course, is from God, but there is much a husband can do to make his wife feel safe and protected. I believe that when a husband continually tells his wife that she is beautiful, when he does his best to affirm her strengths and help her deal with any perceived weaknesses, it reflects in her countenance and makes her feel more secure in the marriage relationship.

✦ BETTY

From day one James was an encourager. I don't know if it was because of his background; he wasn't affirmed as a child, yet he appreciated affirmation so much as an adult. He often said, "I'm going to encourage Betty in the areas I know God wants to cultivate in her life." He has always lifted me up, but I haven't always appreciated it as I should.

When we were first married, I confess that I depended completely on James for my joy, peace, and security, and I expected him to do a lot for me because I was so withdrawn and fearful. I saw James as strong, charismatic, and attractive to other people, but I didn't see myself the same way. I was insecure, so it was easy for me to put myself down. But James wouldn't settle for having me off in a corner feeling down about myself. Instead, he built me up and encouraged me. He told me that I was pretty and that he believed in me. He helped me face my darkest fears as God worked in my heart to overcome them.

I used to be the kind of person who would hold in my emotions, and when James would ask, "What's the matter?" I would answer, "Nothing." Sound familiar? Well, I was actually being dishonest, and James could sense it. So he would say, "Let's talk about it."

As we shared earlier, James has always been forthright and a confronter. There were times early on when he tried to encourage me, and I didn't recognize it as that. For example, I was so timid that I wouldn't call a repairperson to come fix something, and I wouldn't make a long-distance call. At that time you had to use an operator to call long distance, and I would get so nervous that I would ask James to do it instead. He would tell me, "You can do anything that

God enables you to do." He was right, of course, but I didn't always believe him, and I didn't always want to hear what he had to say.

When I began to take my rightful place as a wife and no longer put everything on James, the results were indescribably positive.

BE HONEST AND ENCOURAGING

✦ JAMES

We live in an age when comparing ourselves to other people has become a source of great bondage, self-condemnation, and insecurity. That's why I believe it's important for a husband to build up and encourage his wife. I've told Betty that I want to be her mirror for the rest of her life. When she walks into the room, I want to reflect back the beauty I see in her. Even if she doesn't feel beautiful, she will know she's beautiful before I'm through talking to her. I really believe that one of the reasons Betty looks so youthful and beautiful is because I won't allow her to think of herself any other way.

Please understand that I will not be dishonest with Betty. For example, before we taped our show on the morning I wrote this, she came into the family room several times wearing three or four different outfits. Each time, she asked, "How does this look?"

I was always honest, even when I had to say, "I don't know if that really flatters you. I don't know if that looks right."

Well, when I said that, she turned and rapidly left the room. I had disappointed her. That's not what she wanted to hear. She wanted me to say, "That's awesome. You look great! It's unbelievable." But I have to be honest. Even as she was walking away, I said, "Well, do you want me to tell you the truth, or do you just want me to say that you look great in whatever?"

A minute later she came back into the room wearing other clothes, and this outfit really did look great. And I told her so.

Betty was looking for affirmation, but she was also looking for honesty, and she wanted to know that I cared. She needed to know I wasn't just trying to put her off or get her out of the room so I could get back to what I was doing. One thing I've learned is that when Betty asks, "Does this look all right?" it's a big mistake to say it looks "all right." What woman wants to look just all right? Instead, I tell her, "It looks great!" and I'll often tell her why it looks great and why she looks great and why she makes the clothes look great.

✦ BETTY

I draw comfort from the fact that James makes me feel safe and secure, but I don't take for granted that he will supply those needs in my life. I realize that many women do not have this kind of security, and I am grateful to have a husband who will take on numerous responsibilities, but I can't just take it for granted. I need to tell him through words, acts of love, and physical affection. I need to let him know that he meets my needs and that I want to meet his needs as well. Little words of appreciation and encouragement might seem small, but they are actually very big.

One thing James has faithfully done to encourage me through the years is to call me when he travels. Earlier in our marriage I couldn't always go on the road with him because of my responsibilities at home. When he traveled a lot, I needed to know he was thinking about me. Even though he was busy ministering to people, preaching the gospel, and being a part of changing other people's lives, I needed to know that he remembered he had a wife and family back home who loved him. Although I was busy myself, I thought of him continually. He would call me on the phone at least once a day and sometimes more than that. If he didn't have a chance to call, I knew it wasn't because he wasn't thinking about me. To this day, wherever James is and whatever he is doing, he calls me often.

> *Little words of appreciation and encouragement might seem small, but they are actually very big.*

And I love to encourage James! Even though he is strong, he needs that encouragement, first from the Lord and then from me. Words of affirmation are very important to a man. If you've seen James on television or at one of his speaking engagements, you know he appears strong, forceful, and confident. It might shock some people to hear that he needs encouragement and affirmation, but that is certainly true. Because most men project an image of strength and sometimes can seem too self-assured and confident, it's easy to think they don't want or need encouragement from their wife. But all men need encouragement, and James is no exception.

✦ JAMES

Betty does a great job of encouraging me! For example, she knows I want to hear the truth about my effectiveness after I've spoken at an event. I'll always ask her, "How did I do?" If she needs to correct me, she will, and I won't be offended. I get tickled by how she will sit up front while I'm speaking and start making funny signs or gestures at me, like a third-base coach in baseball, but Betty's telling me to get my hair out of my eyes, or wipe the spit from a corner of my mouth, or adjust my tie.

One time I walked out of a movie theater with one pant leg wadded up and stuck on the top of my boot. When Betty noticed it, she smiled and said, "You look like a bum!" She wasn't putting me down. She was saying, "Hey, you're in public, and people know you, so straighten out your pant leg." We laughed all the way to the car about how prim-and-proper Betty had just gone to the movie with a bum.

That's the kind of relationship we have. We will not put each other down. When I've failed—and believe me, I fail—I couldn't ask for a greater friend, a greater life raft, a stronger shoulder to lean on than Betty. But the happiness in our marriage hasn't sprung from always meeting each other's expectations. On the contrary, we both have failed many times to live up to the other's expectations. But even in those disappointments, rather than adding to the load of the shortcoming or failure, we immediately begin to try to unload the boat, lighten each other's load, and lift each other up.

This will continue to be the practice and pursuit of our lives. If we get out of kilter in our relationship, even for a few moments, it won't be long before we're once again pulling together, going in the same direction, trying to be each other's best friend and greatest source of encouragement.

✦ BETTY

When God began to build confidence in my heart, along with James's encouragement, I began to change. By not trusting God and ignoring what others say to us, we can really miss opportunities to grow and be uplifted by other people.

No one is harder on a woman than she is on herself when she looks in the mirror, especially in a dressing room where the lighting is usually unflattering. She can see all her imperfections. With pictures of so many thin, beautiful women in airbrushed ads, it's hard to walk out of a dressing room and feel encouraged. Also, some women battle their weight, especially after having children. Not surprisingly, a husband's encouragement can promote a woman's desire and drive to take care of herself and always look her best. A simple comment such as "Honey, you'll always be beautiful to me" can go a long way.

I am even more inspired to maintain my weight when James says something flattering about my exercise discipline or the results I'm attaining. The fact that he notices and expresses appreciation for my efforts reinforces my desire to continue working out. Compliments to a woman are really important. She wants to look her best for her husband.

When I get up in the morning, I don't wait long to fix my face and hair. I don't have to look like someone in a style show, but I can look presentable and neat and put on something that makes me feel good about myself. Sometimes after I've gotten dressed, I'll walk in to greet James, and he'll say, "You always look nice, but you look especially nice today." Again, his taking time to notice my appearance makes me feel loved and appreciated.

Enjoy Each Other

✦ James

Another way in which I've learned to encourage Betty is by letting her know I enjoy her company and want to spend time with her. She and I really are inseparable because we genuinely like to be together. If there's something I want to do, such as play a round of golf, spend time in a sporting goods store, or work on something in our ministry, Betty never makes me feel as if I shouldn't do it. She always encourages me to go, and I do the same for her. We can be generous in that way toward each other because we both know we'd rather be together most of the time.

We've taken an interest in what interests the other person, and we get great pleasure from participating with each other in the things that we love. Believe it or not, I'm a world-class shopper when it comes to looking for household items or clothes for Betty. When we go shopping together, I often encourage her to try on things she might not consider. If I see something I think might look good on her, I'll tell her. She invariably buys more when I go with her, because I help her find things she might have passed over or not noticed.

However, I know many women might not want their husband to shop with them. Sometimes Betty will say, "I need to do some shopping, and I don't want to be rushed. You'd probably drop out before I got through, so I'd like to go alone."

Enjoy Each Other's Interests

During our years together, Betty has become very interested in sports. She is actually a bigger football and basketball fan than I am—and she even likes ice hockey. Now that we've become close friends with Katie and Josh Hamilton, she's also a Texas Rangers baseball fan.

And Betty never gives up on her teams. I have to smile when I think, *Here's* a girl who, when I met her, didn't know what a first down was or a three-point basket or a hat trick, and now she has a wealth of sports knowledge. And it happened because she took an interest in my interests, and then she discovered, "Hey, this is fun for me too."

Betty and I both love nature, but we used to love it in different ways. I've always liked to get out into God's creation, observe wildlife, and hunt and fish. Betty has always preferred to look out a window or sit on a porch to enjoy the display of natural beauty around her.

As we've learned to appreciate each other's interests in our lifelong commitment, we've come to love what the other person loves. Now I take pleasure in sitting on the porch with Betty, enjoying the nature around us, and she enjoys fishing and hunting with me (which now have turned into mostly photo and video opportunities). Betty often rushes into the house exclaiming, "You have to see what I just caught on video!" She never dreamed she could have so much fun in the great outdoors, watching deer, birds, bobcats, and other animals in the wild.

✦ BETTY

That's right. Initially, I became a big sports fan and ventured outdoors more because I took an interest in the things James enjoyed. In the process, I discovered that I enjoyed many of those things myself.

I think it is very important for a wife to take an interest in the things that interest her husband, whether it's sports, the outdoors, or his latest big idea. You don't necessarily have to do everything he likes to do, but it's very important to your husband that you take an interest in what he's doing.

If you find you enjoy some of the same things, that's great. But even if you don't, you can still go a long way toward establishing the heart connection and intimacy you desire if you'll notice what he's doing and listen to him when he talks about his activities or ideas. I never knew that watching sporting events or spending time outdoors could be so much fun, because I had never tried it.

And I never knew that I could actually enjoy being on television. Believe me, when James first presented the idea to me, I was terrified. But since I was willing to listen to him and to try new things, and because we get to do television together, it has all turned out well. We've both matured, and our relationship has grown stronger every year. Again, the specific activities aren't what is important. What's important is that I was willing to enter James's world while seeking to encourage and support him in the things he enjoyed or was called to do.

> *It's very important to your husband that you take an interest in what he's doing.*

✦ JAMES

Betty loves the outdoors and watching wildlife, which she never thought she would enjoy until she sat next to me one day and saw several deer grazing on a hillside. As a general rule, we try to understand why the other person enjoys something. And even if we don't quite get into it ourselves, we don't discourage each other from enjoyable pursuits. Instead, we build each other up and cheer each other on.

SPIRITUAL LEADERSHIP

✦ BETTY

God's Word says that the husband is to be the leader of the home, but that doesn't mean he is to lord it over his wife or treat her like a servant. Being the leader of the home is a big responsibility, as it provides a spiritual covering for the other members of the household. I have the satisfaction of knowing that James is my covering, and I need to let him know that I appreciate his being a covering in my life. It allows me to be who God created me to be as an individual, a wife, and a mother. It frees me up to allow God to develop characteristics in me and for me to be strong as well.

In many marriages it seems that the wife is the one concerned about spiritual issues, and yet she desires that her husband become the one who leads. How wives approach this very sensitive issue is so important.

If you don't feel that your husband is the spiritual leader of your home, realize that you can't push spiritual leadership down his throat, and you don't want to make him feel inadequate. Instead, I think you have to start with your own heart by asking God, "What changes do I need to make that will be an example to my husband and give him a hunger for a more meaningful relationship with You and a desire to love You with his whole heart?" This is the approach we have to take if we want to see positive changes.

In our relationship James was the one who first had a spiritual awakening and a very real, personal relationship with Christ. At first it was kind of overwhelming. I had grown up in the church, and he had come from a rough background, yet God gripped his heart and truly transformed him.

If James had started nagging me about my spiritual walk, I would have retreated even deeper into my shell. Instead, he just loved me and allowed God to do the work in my heart.

It's important to realize that we have to give God time. His timetable is not the same as ours. We get impatient, but the fact is, we would miss some important lessons God wants to teach us if everything happened instantly. Most of the things that have become meaningful in my life started small and then through the years developed into the biggest blessings I could ever imagine.

It's important to realize that we have to give God time.

So we need God-given patience, and we need to realize that pressing or nagging doesn't help at all. Your husband is much more likely to be drawn to God if he sees the life of Christ lived out through you. As the apostle Peter said:

> Wives, be submissive to your own husbands so that even if any of them
> are disobedient to the word, they may be won without a word by the be-

THE POWER OF ENCOURAGEMENT

havior of their wives, as they observe your chaste and respectful behavior.
Your adornment must not be merely external—braiding the hair, and
wearing gold jewelry, or putting on dresses; but let it be the hidden person of the heart, with the imperishable quality of a gentle and quiet
spirit, which is precious in the sight of God. (1 Peter 3:1–4, NASB)

Most likely, spiritual changes won't happen according to your schedule. But
if your husband sees that what you're getting from God's Word and from your
relationship with Him is real, it will have an impact on him. He isn't going to
grow spiritually if you gossip about him or pressure him about his relationship
with God or make him feel inadequate for not measuring up to your standard.
If you're tempted to nag your husband about spiritual matters, choose to pray
for him instead. Prayer is the key for transforming your own heart as well as
your husband's.

To be quite honest, all of the meaningful practices we have shared in this
book have been inspired by our personal relationship with God. These principles work when they are applied, but we need a supernatural ability to live them
out when facing the trials that will surely come. It is good to pray for the best
on behalf of your mate, desiring for God to change your spouse's heart, but you
must be willing to start by allowing God to first remove the log in your own eye.[1]
If you will allow God to change you first and trust Him to make your relationship beautiful, He will do wonders in your life and in your marriage.

A FIRM FOUNDATION

✦ JAMES

We do not have the power or privilege of choosing the challenges we will face
in life. They are not only unpredictable but unexpected and often unwanted.
They will continually come far too fast and furiously. But know this: there is a
foundation on which we can build the house, the relationship, our marriage, and
the future that will withstand every storm we face. There is a shelter from the

storm—a solid Rock, a Counselor, Comforter, Guide, and Friend—to all who trust Him as the perfect Father.

On our television program, *Life Today,* we talk to many guests who have overcome the "perform storm" and every challenge thrown in their path. Perhaps we could serve as a source of continual inspiration to you on your journey and in your marriage. (Please visit our Web site, www.lifetoday.org, for additional information concerning guests and topics or to view programs and discover helpful resources.)

> *We do not have the power or privilege of choosing the challenges we will face in life.*

Betty and I really do live in love. Our lives overflow with joy, and we are crazy about each other. After fifty years and after facing all the challenges that have come our way, our exciting adventure has become even more exhilarating. All that we have faced—the unexpected and the failures—would have been so difficult without a genuine relationship with a God who is truly alive. We have that relationship, and you can have it too. The joy we experience is not for a privileged few. It is for you and your marriage.

Betty and I have each other, and we have our children and grandchildren. All are very special, but they are not our source of joy. We have nice things, but they do not have us. By God's grace, we truly possess our possessions. We have problems, but our God and Father is so much greater than the problems are. Our God is your God. We challenge you to get to know Him, trust Him, and love Him, and you will come to know each other in ways you never imagined. You will become a living expression and visible demonstration of what Jesus prayed on your behalf. You will be an answer to the prayer of Jesus. Wow!

I am praying not only for these disciples but also for all who will ever believe in me through their message. I pray that *they will all be one, just as you and I are one*—as you are in me, Father, and I am in you....

May they experience such perfect unity that the world will know that you sent me and that you love them as much as you love me. (John 17:20–21, 23, emphasis added)

Think of it: God loves you, your spouse, and those you love as much as He loves Jesus, His only Son! Receive it, release it like a river, and, yes, you will truly be continually living in love.

FOR REFLECTION AND DISCUSSION

In what ways do you encourage your spouse? How does your spouse encourage you?

What activities do you and your husband enjoy doing together?

What might you do to make God even more the solid foundation of your marriage?

STUDY GUIDE

MAKING THE MOST OF EACH SESSION

This six-session study guide is designed to be used *after* you have read the chapters designated for each session. However, if you are studying *Living in Love* in a group setting and have not yet read chapters 1–3, when the first session starts, please participate anyway!

While doing this study, keep the goals of each session in mind: to contemplate and pray about what you are learning, and apply the truths of God's Word to your life. As you read and reflect on each chapter, feel free to jot down notes and highlight passages that speak to and challenge your life. Ask the Lord to reveal insights so you will benefit even more from each session's discussions.

If group participants want to move more slowly through one or more sessions, simply adjust the reading assignments and use of questions accordingly.

INTRODUCTION AND GENERAL FEEDBACK

At the start of each session, discuss answers or updates to prayer from previous sessions and then pray together. Next, invite someone to read the brief introduction aloud to highlight the focus of the discussion. The leader should then encourage participants to ask questions and share any "aha" moments, insights, or comments arising from their personal study of the specific chapters within *Living in Love*.

ANTICIPATE WHAT GOD WILL DO

Living in Love focuses on practical ways through which you can build a stronger, growing lifelong commitment to your spouse. It is quite likely that group participants represent a variety of backgrounds and marital experiences. That's great! Focus on these three prerequisites for group participation: (1) a humble desire to grow in Christ and learn from His Word, (2) hearts and minds truly open to what God may reveal through the Robisons' insights into marriage and His Word, and (3) a commitment to interact gently and respectfully with one another.

If participants have differing opinions on a particular topic, respond graciously to one another. Listen attentively to what others have to say. Review pertinent Bible verses and keep focused on the Bible as the final word on an issue. **If a participant continues to struggle with a concept, or tension begins to build within the group,** agree to pray about the issue and report back as the next session begins.

Above all, remember that you are on a journey of discovery together. Trust the Holy Spirit to reveal truth and, if necessary, change hearts and minds—the heart or mind He changes may be your own!

REFLECT ON THE QUESTIONS

The reflection and discussion questions are designed to help you relate to and discuss each session's main topics rather than **eliciting predetermined ("right") answers**. Therefore, do not race through questions. Take your time. If you don't get through all the questions in a particular session, relax and trust God. Allow the Holy Spirit to work and minister uniquely through you and other participants.

Key Verse

Each session features one theme verse related to the session's content. Read the verse aloud. Participants using different Bible translations might also read the verse aloud so the group receives greater understanding. Try to memorize the verses.

Close Each Session in Prayer

Be sure to leave enough time at the end of each session for prayer! Praying together at the end of each session powerfully adds effectiveness, authenticity, and relevance to previous discussion. And remember that God not only listens to your prayers but He responds to them!

Prepare for the Next Session

Between each session, be sure to read the assigned chapters of *Living in Love*. That way, you will be prepared and be even more sensitive to what God may reveal.

Session 1

Expectations and Heart Issues

(Chapters 1, 2, and 3)

INTRODUCTION

Before your wedding day, you had certain hopes, dreams, and expectations of what your marriage would be like...including how this other person whom you loved so deeply would meet your needs.

Whether you are in or out of a significant relationship, you have ideas of what a marital relationship should be like. And the fact that the person you married—or may marry—will be different from you in some ways adds to the special challenges of marriage.

No matter how wonderful the journey of marriage can be, somewhere along the way your relationship with your mate will experience challenges. Both of you will be tested.

To illustrate, let's compare a marital challenge to a slowly leaking tire as you drive down the road. When challenge arises, you could worry and do nothing—angrily ignore the problem and keep driving. Or you could trust the

Protector, who is looking out for your marriage, and take the necessary actions to get your relationship back on track—in effect, fix and inflate the tire. Only you can decide.

Regardless of particular issues you face in marriage, God is with you. With His help and your heart-determined effort, your marriage can improve. Challenges you face can become opportunities to make your marriage better—and even *great*!

REFLECTION AND DISCUSSION

1. James writes, "Instead of trying to change your mate, it is best to allow God to shape *you*. He's the only One with the power to bring meaningful change to your life that will stand the test of time and circumstances." Do you agree or disagree? Why?

2. How do you tend to respond when you face relational challenges and blowouts with your mate? Why?

3. How important a role do you believe God should have in marriage?

4. Why do you think opposites often marry one another? Which strengths and weaknesses occur as a result?

5. On a scale of one (low) to ten (high), how willing are you to make your marriage the best it can be—even if it means

honestly facing tough issues and allowing God to change your heart?

6. Why is sincere change and inner transformation that starts within your own heart much more important to your marriage than following a formula for a better marriage or trying to change your mate?

7. What are some specific ways through which you can cultivate sincere "heart change" within yourself that will help you become a better person and therefore a better mate?

KEY VERSE

All things are possible with God. —Mark 10:27 (NIV)

PRAYER

Dear Lord, thank You for being with us during our journey of marriage, for helping us discover opportunities and face challenges. In Your strength, enable each of us to open our hearts and minds to Your truth and to trust You to guide us toward even stronger marriages. In Jesus's name we pray. Amen.

FOR NEXT TIME

Read chapters 4, 5, 6, and 7 of *Living in Love*.

Session 2

Committed to Each Other: The Glue of Marriage Is Unbreakable Devotion

(Chapters 4, 5, 6, and 7)

INTRODUCTION

Success in marriage starts with a commitment to build the best marriage possible and to do whatever it takes to live in love. We can't do this on our own without God—and we are not meant to do so.

Commitment—unbreakable and exclusive devotion to one's mate—is a key ingredient in building and maintaining a vibrant, fulfilling marriage. It creates safety, and safety in turn creates a climate in which trust, teamwork, and unity grow. Your commitment to love and care for your mate *will* be tested, but such commitment provides great rewards.

Marriage is an unconditional, unbreakable covenant. Yet some people view marriage as a contract that can be renegotiated, broken, or amended and that seeks to protect rights and limit responsibilities.

We need to remain committed to our mates, not allowing other people or activities to keep us from making our mates a priority. It's easy for us to hold back, to avoid complete commitment to our mates because of hurt or a desire to hide our "ugly stuff." All of us bring baggage into our marriages that will surface no matter how well we disguise or hide it. Sometimes we start building our marriages on foundations of distrust, for example. These kinds of things cause us to be less committed to our covenantal marital relationships.

In contrast, strong commitment pushes us beyond fear and frustration, stretching us as we each deal with inevitable challenges of marriage in God-pleasing ways and make firm, daily decisions to honor our mates and remain attuned to their thoughts and feelings.

REFLECTION AND DISCUSSION

1. To which (positive and negative) things or people have you demonstrated commitment? (Be honest!) What do these commitments reveal about you? about your loyalty to your mate?

2. Why are differences between a contract and a covenant important in understanding biblical marriage?

3. How might you demonstrate more covenantal commitment to your spouse? (Ideas: listening, respecting your partner's beliefs, remaining devoted, doing special acts, forsaking all others.)

4. What kinds of things squeeze out the time you spend with your

mate? Why does your calendar reveal a great deal about your allegiances?

5. When we self-protect and do not completely engage with our mate and give everything we have to the marital relationship, what happens? Why?

6. How might your marriage improve if you ask yourself, *What things attracted me to my mate? Are they still there—maybe hidden? How can I rekindle and rediscover them? What might I more fully develop and establish within myself?*

7. Why are the intentions of our spouses, what stems from their hearts, important to keep in mind when they say or do offensive or disappointing things? Do you find it easy or difficult to look beyond words and actions to see your mate's intentions of the heart? Why?

8. In what positive ways can we face baggage—emotional states, habits, hang-ups, vices, feelings about ourselves, personality traits—that each of us brings into marriage (i.e., Bible-based counseling, talking honestly with other people, forgiving and receiving forgiveness, prayer, etc.)? If you feel comfortable, share an example from your life.

9. What happens when we break our commitments to our mates—through workaholism, lust, greed, anger, infidelity, pornography, substance abuse, pride, compulsive spending…and other ways?

10. In what types of broken-commitment circumstances might it be necessary for a mate to receive outside assistance, counseling, or intervention?

KEY VERSE

May the God of hope fill you with all joy and peace as you trust in him, so that you may overflow with hope by the power of the Holy Spirit. —Romans 15:13 (NIV)

PRAYER

Dear Lord, thank You for helping us recognize anew our need to be completely committed to our mates and for Your love and power that bring hope and restoration into our marriages. Empower us to totally submit to You and strive to build and rebuild our relationships.

FOR NEXT TIME

Read chapters 8, 9, and 10 of *Living in Love.*

Session 3

Communication

(Chapters 8, 9, and 10)

INTRODUCTION

Effective verbal and nonverbal communication between a husband and wife not only makes commitment, trust, and concern visible in marriage, it is essential to living in love. We all need an open channel for direct communication—talking and listening, giving and receiving.

Think of the ways by which we communicate to our mates—gestures, tone, facial expressions, posture, eye contact… But *what* are we communicating—often without words?

For example, when a disagreement arises, do you seek to love, understand, and listen to your mate's heart? to be clear, open, and honest? to view him or her as a team member on the same side? to pray together about a difficult issue and trust God to help you work things out?

Key ingredients in effective communication include being aware of how we speak and being willing to diagnose and overcome communication difficulties. Sometimes we will need to confront our mates in healthy ways, lovingly and honestly dealing with frustrations and anger in order to avoid the possibility of serious marital damage.

During this session, we will consider effective ways to communicate with our mates, loving ways to confront and achieve resolution, and why confession between a husband and his wife brings healing, restoration, and strength.

REFLECTION AND DISCUSSION

COMMUNICATING

1. What kinds of verbal and nonverbal communication have you established in your marriage, and what impact have they had—positively and negatively—on each of you?

2. James writes, "If we're going to thrive, we must approach our commitment to each other as an act of teamwork....[and] issues and hurts must be addressed." Why is this perspective important in keeping lines of marital communication open? What does Ephesians 4:26–27 reveal?

3. How can you encourage successful communication with your mate—and keep communication channels open?

CONFRONTING

1. Betty writes, "Communicating well with your spouse will at times mean gently pointing out something that bothers you."

What are some ways in which we can lovingly confront our mates—and ways in which we create hurt, self-protection, and other sinful by-products?

2. James writes, "To Betty and me, *confrontation* is a positive word." Why is loving and honest confrontation between a married couple necessary—and a key part of necessary relationship building?

Confessing

1. James writes, "We all have stickers in our lives. Whether it's an addiction, an attitude, a habit, a past pain, or a current problem, it's something that is hurting us and preventing us from walking in freedom and unity in our relationships. Confession is the act of revealing our stickers to another person and saying, 'Would you help me get this out of my life?'" Which "stickers" are in your life? Why are such confessions of problems, challenges, weaknesses, and temptations both scary and healing?

2. Why is it important for husbands and wives to learn how to wisely "share each other's burdens" (Galatians 6:2) in love, and how does confessing our anger, lust, addictions, jealousy—within the safety of loving marriages—enable us to bring healing, strength, and confidence into our marriages?

KEY VERSE

Reckless words pierce like a sword, but the tongue of the
wise brings healing. —Proverbs 12:18 (NIV)

PRAYER

Dear Lord, thank You for hearing our prayers and helping us to bring togetherness and unity into our marriages. Enable us to communicate better, and as we grow spiritually, increase our willingness to confess to You and to our spouses our weaknesses, temptations, and sins so we can grow stronger as couples. And guide us as we learn to pray together and receive healing, forgiveness, and restoration. In Jesus's name we pray. Amen.

FOR NEXT TIME

Read chapters 12, 13, and 14 of *Living in Love*.

Session 4

Three Challenges: Money, Parenting, Sex

(Chapters 12, 13, and 14)

INTRODUCTION

Every marital journey will face challenges. The question is not, Will our marriages face challenges? but, When marital challenges come, how effectively will we deal with them?

During this session, we will consider three challenges that most couples face in marriage: money, parenting, and sexual intimacy.

In building a strong and lasting marriage, one of the first and most important issues every couple must agree on is how to manage their money. So many marriages on the road to ruin typically experience financial problems, so it's vital that each of us recognize what God says about money. If you have not lived below your means or built your financial future on the solid rock of your commitment to God, it's not too late to start making wise financial decisions—that may include reading Bible-based books on family finances.

Parenting, another great responsibility many couples take on, is designed to be a team effort between husband and wife. What if you are divorced or alone for other reasons in your parenting? Fortunately, all types of parents benefit from applying proven biblical parenting principles. We'll consider a few of them during this session.

The topic of sex usually causes people to squirm, yet within marriage, sex is an essential part of marital intimacy and serves to promote complete oneness (see Genesis 2:24). Rightly understood, sex is a natural, exciting, and beautiful act when practiced in the context of marriage based on lifelong commitment, mutual trust, and mutual concern.

REFLECTION AND DISCUSSION

MANAGING FINANCES

1. Look up the following verses and discuss what they reveal about money and our attitudes toward it: Philippians 4:19; 2 Corinthians 9:7–9; 11:28; 1 Timothy 6:9–10, 17; Proverbs 3:9; Ecclesiastes 5:10; Matthew 6:21.

2. Which of these principles do you find most difficult to apply, and why?

- Live within your means.
- Trust and honor God, who promises to supply our needs.
- Do not build your self-worth on the foundation of money.
- Reduce or eliminate nonmortgage debt; invest only in equity-producing investments.

- Choose to make God, not things, your source of contentment.

3. Describe situations—positive and negative—through which you have learned important truths about money, God, and family finances.

PARENTING

1. Why is it important for children to see their parents deal with conflict, day-to-day decision making, and other aspects of family life using principles of commitment, trust, and communication?

2. In light of Deuteronomy 11:18–20, what are the key differences between just telling children what to do/what not to do and diligently instructing them in the proper ways to live as they have opportunities to practice, fail, learn, and grow?

SEX WITHIN MARRIAGE

1. Contrast prevalent cultural perspectives of sex with 1 Corinthians 6:15–20, including—as you feel comfortable sharing—thoughts on why God has established these boundaries.

2. Betty writes, "[Sexual] ecstasy apart from commitment, trust, and mutual care and concern is a dead-end street. In fact, it's quite damaging. Sex is designed to be an expression of commitment and genuine intimacy that only a husband and wife can

share. In any other context, it eventually and inevitably degrades our humanity." Do you agree or disagree? Why?

3. What sexual danger zones do we face in everyday life, and how might a married couple deal with them—including setting safe boundaries? To aid in discussion, read 1 Corinthians 10:12–13; Matthew 15:19; 1 Corinthians 6:18–20; Ephesians 5:3; Colossians 3:5.

KEY VERSE

Guard yourself in your spirit, and do not break faith
with the wife of your youth. —Malachi 2:15

PRAYER

God, You are always with us and always willing to help us build stronger marriages. It isn't easy for us to deal with such issues as money, parenting, and sex. Thank You that we can call out to You for comfort and wisdom. Thank You for giving us Your Word and its lasting principles to guide us. As we commit ourselves to our marriages, we remember that You are so committed to us that You sent Your Son, Jesus, to die for our sins. May we continue to draw closer to You each day. In Jesus's name, amen.

FOR NEXT TIME

Read chapter 15 of *Living in Love*.

Session 5

The Invisible Enemy

(Chapter 15)

INTRODUCTION

Many Christians are unaware that a hidden, evil force in the spiritual realm is determined to create chaos and attack them, their mates, and their children. Using deception, distraction, temptation, and other strategies, this enemy—Satan—and his evil spirits often succeed. Satan especially hates the institution of marriage, which is to serve as a picture of the intimate relationship between Jesus and His followers.

Not surprisingly, the Enemy attacks our intimacy with God, seeking to isolate us from our Defender and the ultimate source of our power. Satan also tries to damage or destroy intimacy between a husband and wife—the unity that God designed. So, this evil being attacks both the family structure within society and the church—the family of God.

Satan is a fierce enemy who hates true love and life. A relentless predator, he knows if he can drive a wedge into a marriage and create distance, friction, and discouraging issues, both spouses are more vulnerable.

During this session, we will learn about spiritual warfare recorded and described in the Bible and some of the ways in which this warfare is directed at our marriages.

REFLECTION AND DISCUSSION

1. After discussing what the Bible reveals in Matthew 6:13 and 1 Peter 5:8, read these verses aloud: James 4:7–8, 10; 1 Peter 5:6, 8–9; 1 John 4:4; 2 Corinthians 2:11; 10:3–5; Psalm 40:2.

2. From whom does our hope and power come? In what specific ways do these verses relate to our marriages, which are under constant bombardment by evil ones in the spiritual realm?

3. Which spiritual weapons are available to us, and what do we need to recognize in order for God's supernatural power to lift us up, provide a firm foundation, and enable us to stand firm against Satan's schemes? (See Ephesians 6:10–18.)

4. Why do you think the authors included this chapter on spiritual warfare, and why is it easy for many of us to act as if Satan does not exist rather than recognizing the reality of spiritual warfare and the influence of unclean spirits?

5. If you feel comfortable doing so, share ways in which Satan and his evil ones have attacked you—using such tools as pressure,

fear, condemnation, accusation—at points of weakness that likely correspond to your strengths. How have these attacks affected your marriage and God's overall purpose for your life?

6. What changes might God desire you to make so that you will receive the true freedom and power He offers so that you can effectively challenge the Evil One when he tries to undermine your marriage?

7. Why is it important for us to understand that in this lifetime we will never escape spiritual warfare and that resisting the Enemy is a lifetime commitment?

KEY VERSE

Finally, be strong in the Lord and in his mighty power.
Put on the full armor of God so that you can take your stand
against the devil's schemes. —Ephesians 6:10–11 (NIV)

PRAYER

God, thank You for bringing us together as husbands and wives who now invite You to help us strengthen our marriages. Teach us not only to remain aware of the Enemy but to resist him using the armor You describe in Ephesians 6. Knowing that the Enemy hates marriages built on biblical foundations, we call out for Your help. May we trust You more, submit ourselves to You, and allow

You to mold and shape us to be the kind of mates we need to be in order for our marriages to be what You want them to be. We yield ourselves to the abounding fullness of Your Spirit, who will fill us with Your power and fruit. In Jesus's name we pray. Amen.

FOR NEXT TIME

Read chapters 11 and 16 of *Living in Love*.

Session 6

❦

Wise Counsel and the Power of Encouragement

(Chapters 11 and 16)

INTRODUCTION

We all face difficult challenges at times, and when marital commitment and trust are challenged and positive solutions and results are fleeting, we have a key choice: we can keep trying—often without success—on our own, or we can willingly admit our failures and weaknesses and pursue outside help and wise spiritual counsel (as James and Betty did).

Sadly, brothers and sisters in Christ to whom we turn for advice may provide little or no help. Even worse, they may scoff at us, gossip about us, be unwilling to stand with us during our times of need, provide unwise and unsolicited opinions, or respond in other unloving ways.

That's why it's important for each of us to pray for God's guidance when we reach points at which outside counsel is needed in our marriages. Often using the recommendations of other Christ followers and counseling agencies, He will direct us to the right person(s) in whom we can confide.

Whatever counsel you receive—from a Christian leader, a godly counselor, a Christian friend, etc.—be sure to check it against what the Bible says and the level of peace in your heart. True, godly counsel will reflect the truth of Scripture.

REFLECTION AND DISCUSSION

1. John Donne wrote, "No man is an island, entire of itself." Yet why do many married couples try to live as if they are islands, just surviving, when they could receive practical and godly wisdom and start thriving?

2. Read John 14:15–17, 26; John 15:26–27; and John 16:4–7. What did Jesus reveal about the guidance and help of our Advocate—the Holy Spirit?

3. Respond to this statement: "*Never* talk about your marital challenges with someone of the opposite sex, even if he or she is a close friend. All too often this type of counsel leads to an inappropriate emotional relationship."

4. How can we know whether the outside counsel we receive is truly wise and godly?

5. What specific things can we do to affirm and encourage our mates and help them deal with any perceived weaknesses? How

do these kinds of loving attitudes and actions provide a sense of security in a marital relationship?

6. Although we can do much to encourage our mates, why must each of us recognize that only God can ultimately provide our security and supply our needs?

7. The Robisons agree that their personal relationship with God has inspired all the meaningful practices they shared in this book. In what way(s) is your relationship with God inspiring you and your spouse to build a stronger marriage?

Key Verse

Encourage each other and build each other up, just as you are already doing. —1 Thessalonians 5:11

Prayer

Dear Lord, thank You for the opportunities we have had to learn about our individual relationships with You and our relationships with our mates. Please continue to guide us in learning to receive Your deep love and to keep expressing Your love in even deeper ways—in our marriages and wherever we go. May we remain mindful of Your constant presence with us and continue to turn to You and Your Word. Thank You for the practical tips and encouragement we have received from *Living in Love* and these sessions. In Jesus's name. Amen.

NOTES

Chapter 3: Key Ingredients

1. See John 5:1–15.
2. Jean Sulivan, *Morning Light: The Spiritual Journal of Jean Sulivan,* trans. Joseph Cunneen and Patrick Gormally (New York: Paulist Press, 1988), 21.

Chapter 4: Committed to Each Other

1. Adapted from Robert Morris and Debbie Morris, *The Blessed Marriage* (Southlake, TX: Gateway Church, 2006), 26–38.
2. Ephesians 5:25, NASB.
3. Mark 10:27.
4. See John 10:10; Isaiah 61:1.

Chapter 6: Baggage: The Junk in the Trunk

1. See John 4:7–42.
2. See John 8:1–11.
3. See Jeremiah 2:13.

Chapter 7: Broken Commitments

1. See Zephaniah 3:17, NIV; Isaiah 63:1.
2. See Psalm 103:4, NIV.
3. See 2 Samuel 11; 1 Samuel 16:1–13; 1 Samuel 13:13–14; 1 Samuel 17.
4. 2 Samuel 11:11.
5. See 2 Samuel 12:14–19.
6. See 2 Samuel 12:24; 1 Kings 4:29–31.
7. See Mark 14:66–72; John 18:10–11.

8. See John 21:15–19.
9. See Acts 2:14–41.

Chapter 8: Communication

1. Albert Mehrabian and Susan R. Ferris, "Inference of Attitude from Nonverbal Communication in Two Channels," *Journal of Counseling Psychology* 31, no. 1 (1967): 248–52.
2. 1 Peter 3:4.
3. See 1 Peter 3:1–2.
4. 2 Timothy 2:16–17.
5. Caroline Leaf, *Who Switched Off My Brain? Controlling Toxic Thoughts and Emotions,* rev. ed. (Nashville: Thomas Nelson, 2009).
6. Ephesians 4:3, NASB.

Chapter 9: Confrontation

1. See Ephesians 4:14–16.
2. Matthew 6:12.

Chapter 10: Confession

1. Galatians 6:1–3.
2. See Matthew 18:19.
3. Squire Rushnell and Louise DuArt, *Couples Who Pray: The Most Intimate Act Between a Man and a Woman* (Nashville: Thomas Nelson, 2007), 12.
4. Rushnell and DuArt, *Couples Who Pray,* 9–11.
5. Proverbs 5:22, NASB.
6. 2 Samuel 12:11, NIV.

Chapter 11: Counsel

1. See Luke 11:11–13.

2. See John 14:16–18; 16:13.

3. Acts 17:11, NASB.

4. Matthew 7:7.

Chapter 12: Money

1. See Philippians 4:19.

2. See 2 Corinthians 9:7 9.

3. 1 Timothy 6:17, NKJV.

4. See Matthew 7:24–27.

5. See 1 Timothy 6:17.

6. Matthew 6:21, NKJV.

7. See, for example, Dave Ramsey, *The Total Money Makeover: A Proven Plan for Financial Fitness* (Nashville: Thomas Nelson, 2003). Ron Blue and Jeremy L. White, *Surviving Financial Meltdown: Confident Decisions in an Uncertain World* (Wheaton, IL: Tyndale, 2009); Ron Blue with Jeremy White, *The New Master Your Money* (Chicago: Moody, 2004); Ron Blue and Jeremy L. White, *Faith-Based Family Finances* (Wheaton, IL: Tyndale, 2008); Larry Burkett, *Debt-Free Living: Eliminating Debt in a New Economy* (Chicago: Moody, 2010); Larry Burkett, *How to Manage Your Money* (Chicago: Moody, 2002); Howard Dayton, *Your Money Counts: The Biblical Guide to Earning, Spending, Saving, Investing, Giving, and Getting Out of Debt* (Wheaton, IL: Tyndale, 1997); Howard Dayton, *Money and Marriage God's Way* (Chicago: Moody, 2009); and Randy Alcorn, *Money, Possessions, and Eternity,* rev. ed. (Wheaton, IL: Tyndale, 2003).

Chapter 13: Parenting

1. Ephesians 4:3, NASB.

Chapter 14: Sex

1. Susan E. Barker, "Cuddle Hormone: Research links oxytocin and socio-sexual behaviors," www.oxytocin.org/cuddle-hormone/.

Chapter 15: The Invisible Enemy

1. 2 Timothy 1:7.
2. See 2 Timothy 1:7.
3. See Matthew 26:33; Mark 14:29.
4. See Ephesians 6:16; "fiery darts" is from the New King James Version; "flaming missiles" is from the Amplified Bible.

Chapter 16: The Power of Encouragement

1. See Luke 6:41–42.

RESOURCES ON MARRIAGE AND FAMILY

As we indicated earlier, we do not consider ourselves experts on marriage and family issues. We appreciate the many other authors who write on these topics. Two authors in particular, though, have meant a great deal to us: Robert Morris, the pastor of our home church, and Jimmy Evans, a longtime friend. Because we have such great respect for them, we have listed several of their resources first. After that, we have included a number of books that also offer much insight.

Evans, Jimmy. *Marriage on the Rock: God's Design for Your Dream Marriage.* Dallas: Marriage Today, 1994.

———. *Our Secret Paradise: Seven Secrets for Building a Secure and Satisfying Marriage.* Ventura, CA: Gospel Light, 2006.

Morris, Robert, and Debbie Morris. *The Blessed Marriage: Experiencing Heaven on Earth in Your Marriage.* Southlake, TX: Gateway Church, 2006. Available at www.gatewaypeople.com.

Morris, Robert, and James Robison. *Living Free—Breaking Free from the Cycle of Defeat.* This teaching series on spiritual warfare is available on CD and DVD at Life Outreach International, www.lifetoday.org.

✦ ✦ ✦

Arterburn, Stephen, Fred Stoeker, and Mike Yorkey. *Every Man's Battle: Winning the War on Sexual Temptation One Victory at a Time.* Colorado Springs: WaterBrook, 2000.

Chapman, Gary. *The Five Love Languages: How to Express Heartfelt Commitment to Your Mate.* Chicago: Northfield, 1992, 1995.

Dillow, Linda, and Lorraine Pintus. *Intimate Issues: 21 Questions Christian Women Ask About Sex.* Colorado Springs: WaterBrook, 1999.

Eggerichs, Emerson. *Love and Respect: The Love She Most Desires, the Respect He Desperately Needs.* Nashville: Thomas Nelson, 2004.

Eldredge, John, and Stasi Eldredge. *Captivating: Unveiling the Mystery of a Woman's Soul.* Nashville: Thomas Nelson, 2005.

———. *Love and War: Finding the Marriage You've Dreamed Of.* New York: Doubleday, 2009.

Feldhahn, Shaunti. *For Women Only: What You Need to Know about the Inner Lives of Men.* Sisters, OR: Multnomah, 2004.

Feldhahn, Shaunti and Jeff Feldhahn. *For Men Only: A Straightforward Guide to the Inner Lives of Women.* Sisters, OR: Multnomah, 2006.

Kendrick, Stephen, and Alex Kendrick. *The Love Dare.* Nashville: B & H Publishing, 2008.

Leman, Kevin. *Sheet Music: Uncovering the Secrets of Sexual Intimacy in Marriage.* Carol Stream, IL: Tyndale, 2003.

Mason, Mike. *The Mystery of Marriage, 20th Anniversary Edition: Meditations on the Miracle.* Sisters, OR: Multnomah, 2005.

Rosberg, Gary, and Barbara Rosberg. *Healing the Hurt in Your Marriage.* Carol Stream, IL: Tyndale, 2004.

———. *The 5 Love Needs of Men and Women.* Carol Stream, IL: Tyndale, 2000.

About the Authors

James and Betty Robison met in Pasadena, Texas, at the age of fifteen, while serving in Vacation Bible school. They married four years later on February 23, 1963, and have spent their entire lives in ministry.

For thirty years, James preached the gospel in more than six hundred city-wide crusades. Approximately twenty million people attended those meetings, with more than two million making decisions for Christ.

In the early 1990s, the Lord led James and Betty into an expanded ministry of evangelism and compassion through humanitarian relief. They established Life Outreach International and have been privileged to meet the practical needs of the world's most desperate people while sharing the gospel. The Robisons have inspired the support of missions and relief efforts in approximately fifty countries.

In addition to helping feed more than five hundred thousand children a month in Africa, Life Outreach has already drilled more than twenty-six hundred water wells in thirty nations, built entire neighborhoods in poor and devastated regions, and delivered medicine and clothing to millions around the globe to fulfill Jesus's decree to reach "the least of these."

In 1995, James and Betty began cohosting *Life Today*, an inspirational television program that now broadcasts daily to more than three hundred million households around the world. In response to viewers and friends who have observed the Robisons' joy-filled relationship and asked for their insights on "living in love," James and Betty agreed to put their thoughts and their journey on paper.

The Robisons live in the Fort Worth area. They have three children and eleven grandchildren.